2009

OFFENSIVE LINE COACHES HANDBOOK

FEATURING LECTURES FROM THE 2009 C.O.O.L. CLINIC

Edited by Earl Browning

COACHES CHOICE™

www.coacheschoice.com

ISBN: 978-1-60679-066-3

ISSN: 1945-1172

Telecoach, Inc. Transcription: Kent Browning and Tom Cheaney

Diagrams: John Rice

Book layout and cover design: Bean Creek Studio

Front cover photo: © St. Petersburg Times/ZUMA Press

Back cover photo of Howard Mudd: Indianapolis Colts Public Relations and Media Departments

Special thanks to John Widecan of the University of Cincinnati for taping the lectures.

Coaches Choice
P.O. Box 1828
Monterey, CA 93942
www.coacheschoice.com

Contents

SPEAKER INTRODUCTIONS/COACHING POINTS TO STIMULATE C.O.O.L.

Cincinnati Bengals

Clinic Director Bob Wylie

Before introducing Paul Alexander, the moderator for the Friday night session, I want to give you a brief history of the C.O.O.L. Clinic. Jim McNally was the offensive line coach for the Cincinnati Bengals from 1980 to 1994. In 1990, Jim invited several coaches over to the football complex to visit and talk football. The room was too small to hold everyone; so the next year, we went to Spinney Field to hold the meeting. Then, we grew into what you are going to see here tonight and tomorrow. Jim McNally has really been responsible for the process and growth of this clinic.

Jim retired from the NFL in 2008. Last year was his first year out of coaching. He coached 28 years in the NFL. I have known Jimmy since 1975. I was a junior high school football coach in Rhode Island, and Jimmy was the line coach at Boston College. He has done so much for offensive line coaches throughout the nation. Everyone here knows Jim McNally. He has videos for sale out in the hall that he has made over the years in coaching. He lectures to schools and colleges, and he will help you any way he can. You can call him day or night, and he is willing to talk with you. He is that type of guy.

When he retired, we went out and got him a little gift to celebrate his longevity in the NFL and in coaching for all of those years. So I would like for Jimmy McNally to come up for this award. Jim did not know this was going to happen, but we have a presentation to make to him.

The award has a picture of the mushroom and the inscription reads: *For 28 years a mushroom*, and it includes the dates he served. Let's give him a big round of applause. Jim McNally.

Paul Alexander runs this show on Friday night. I will be around tonight, and I will be the moderator on Saturday. Thank you for your attention.

Paul Alexander (Moderator)

We do have a tight schedule for the three speakers tonight. I thought I would do something a little different this year in that I want to make a few comments about some topics that I feel will stimulate your thoughts about blocking.

When I spoke at the convention this year, I said, "The only place that I give out new information is the C.O.O.L. Clinic." I only talk about new ideas at this clinic, so let me assure you that you will have to think about these topics.

In colleges, I am seeing defenders that are getting better and better at using their hands in rushing the pass protection. When a defender goes inside, we use a technique called a *lift*. The lift is not a punch. The lift is the opposite of a club that we use on the outside rush. The lift is an inside lift with the inside hand.

When a defender goes inside on us, you have heard me say, "Feet before hands." Instead of going feet...hands, I go feet...lift with the hands underneath with the thumbs up. That is a thought.

The University of Connecticut did a great job last year. They ran the ball very well. We studied their film because they had the great running back, obviously. They had a great season and Coach Foley is going to talk about one-back and two-back power plays. Coach Foley. [Editor's Note: Coach Mike Foley's lecture is included in a separate chapter.]

Thank you Coach Foley. Mike talked about the spot so much. You draw a line, and you hit a spot.

We start with the back foot of the quarterback and the outside leg of the end. You draw a line at a 45-degree mark and that is where the spot is located (Diagram #1).

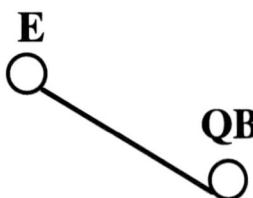

Diagram #1. The Spot

Does the spot always stay the same? No, the spot changes. I do not know why it took me so long to learn this. The stance the rusher is in can affect your spot. Typically, 90 percent of NFL rushers have their outside foot back. The rusher goes one, two, and three. All of his moves are off his third step. So the spot is kind of left where the guy goes on three steps.

There have been a few NFL players that we have had trouble blocking on this setup. One player gave us trouble. He was one of the 10 percent of guys who had his inside foot back. The thing he did was off one and two. What happens if you take a normal set in your spot and he is an inside-foot rusher, he can blow the tackle over on the pass-protection set. The blocker ends up too deep.

My point is this: If the pass rusher has the wrong foot back, we want the tackle to take a shorter step on his pass-protection set. We want to take him on sooner. The difference is this: We know that 90 percent of players have the outside foot back, and the tackle can still set at the 45-degree angle. It does make a difference on which foot is back for the pass rusher. This year, we shut the guy down that we always had a hard time blocking before.

This year, we instituted a new way to introduce the push-pull drill. It is a great drill for balance. When we push on the other man, he tends to lose his balance. We break it down now. We push easy on the man and allow him to keep his balance as he retreats. He has his hands behind his back and he is giving us a target to shoot at on the push. This teaches the players how to squat, how to set their feet, and how to retreat on the block.

The next part of the drill is that you go back and forth. Each man gets a turn of being the blocker and the rusher. The last couple of weeks we have added a lateral push-pull drill to the original drill. We have the rusher grab the shoulders. He will push and pull on the outside shoulders. It is amazing how many people get their shoulders tilted one way or the other. They do not want to move their feet over to keep their weight balanced. The value of the drill, if I go back and forth and side to side, is that the body stays like a cube and it does not tilt sideways or forward. This is how we teach the drill. I think we should have been doing it that way sooner.

Our next speaker is Tom Brattan of the University of Maryland. Tom. [*Editor's Note:* Coach Tom Brattan's lecture is included in a separate chapter.]

Thank you for a great lecture, Tom. You made some excellent points in the presentation. Tom mentioned the Mushroom Society. I want to elaborate about the mushroom for just a minute. Do you know how to kill a mushroom? You put a little detergent in some water and you pour it on the mushroom, and you end up killing it with soap. The phosphates in the soap will kill the mushroom. That means we will have to take out all of the shampoo from the rooms tonight. If we don't take the shampoo out of the rooms, we will not have anyone here in the morning with all of these mushrooms here tonight.

I had a point to make before I tried to make a joke about the mushroom. We have been doing this next drill for a few weeks. We have been doing drills getting ready for our early pre-season practice, which serves us as our spring practice. Perhaps some of you do this drill as well. It is old school for me, and for an NFL coach to do it, but I think it is very good.

We are into training performance. We are also into training players who to block and how to do it, but how to do it in a very competitive situation. This is how we do it.

We have them partner up. We have 25 full-speed pass sets against the pass rushes. You get set and go. You come back, get set, and do it again and again. You come back, get set, and do it again. Obviously, the players are tired when they get back in their stance to go again. We are barking at them to stay down and all the other things you teach them in pass protection.

The next thing we have them do is to drive block a partner for 10 yards. We come back and drive block for another 10 yards. We keep doing the drive block until we reach 100 yards. We have been doing this for the last two weeks. After they get a week off, we bring them back and start teaching them techniques.

There are so many guys working out, and as the games go on and the players start to tire, we see that a lot of them are not in good condition. They do not get into football shape. They do a good job in the weight room and they do a good job running, but they do not do as well in doing the types of drills that condition them for football. The more drills you can get them to do that will help them perform, I think it is a good idea.

Our next speaker is Stacy Searels from the University of Georgia. I have coached a couple of his previous products, and I can tell you, he is a great coach. Coach Searels. [*Editor's Note:* Coach Stacy Searels' lecture is included in a separate chapter.]

Thank you for a great lecture, Stacy. Here we go. The Golden Gate Bridge, like all suspension bridges, is built on an arc (Diagram #2). Why is the suspension bridge built on an arc?

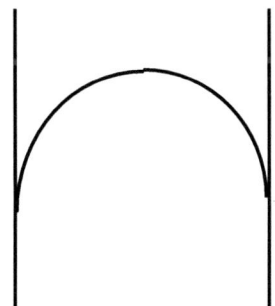

Diagram #2. Suspension Bridge

An engineer issue gives the bridge more strength and stability when it is on an arch than it does when it is on a straight line. That is why they build the bridges with the arch. They can span the distance so well with the arch as opposed to the straight line (Diagram #3).

Diagram #3. Straight Suspension Bridge

How does the bridge building apply to football? Everything we do in football involves leverage. We saw one of the players from the film that Coach Searels showed; I noticed one of his linemen (number 77) who had a great build for blocking because of the arch in his back (Diagram #4). He had a natural way of arching his back. I bet he is going to be a great blocker.

Diagram #4. Arch in the Back

The strong pass blockers do not have a straight up-and-down stance because they do not have enough strength. The blockers who have strength to pass block have their tails up slightly and their backs are arched. The good blockers have this arch in their back. They have a good blocking angle in pass blocking, and they have it in run blocking where they can arch and hit on the rise.

They are like an airplane going in the air on the takeoff. They are like a golf ball going off the club. Any trajectory movement goes up on a gradual plain. It is more of a lifting force that starts out gradually and then goes up a steep rise after it gets the momentum. It is the same lifting force similar to getting leverage in football. When you get those blockers in those positions, make sure they arch their backs. A good way to do that is to tell the blockers to pull their shoulder blades in, so they have a natural arching movement to generate the power. That is kind of fascinating.

We only have one group that has come to sell their wares. Why is this? Because he buys the pizza for the group tonight. He is going to talk for 10 minutes. Matt are you talking, or is David going to do the talking? Ok, David is going to talk about their program which is called *Hudl*.

David Graff: Hudl

Thanks for having us back again this year. We were here last year and showed the Hudl Pro. We had several high schools that used the program last year. In addition, the Nebraska Huskers used our program. Last year, the New York Jets of the NFL used the program as well. Coach Mike Bloomgren is here today. I have asked him to join us at the end of our talk.

Last year as we went around the country, we received a lot of inquiries from the high schools and from smaller colleges. They were facing the same issues that the New York Jets and the Nebraska Huskers were facing. For distributing game film to their players, they said Hudl Pro was better than DVDs. Breaking down film and copying it on a DVD is time-consuming. With Hudl Pro, all of that is set up.

When we first built Hudl Pro, we sat down with Coach Callahan in 2006; we wanted to know what he wanted from the Hudl Pro. He said he wanted to make it possible for all of his players and coaches to be able to see the film wherever they went. The info we demonstrated here last year allows you to view the films from anywhere in the country. The players could log on the TV and see the film from practice or from a game. You can view opponents' film from the scouting films from any area where they were located. They could do a lot of neat things with additional presentations on the TV. In addition, you could consolidate all of the information for viewing at any time or place on the TV.

We have a program now that we are just calling *Hudl*. Our website is: www.hudl.com. We have information available and you can contact us on the website. We have built an online version of the product that starts at $800 per year. It is a device that you can provide game films for all of your players and coaches. You do not have to burn the DVDs. Instead of burning DVDs or waiting to go online to burn your DVD, you can send us the DVD and we will make it available to everyone on your list to open the program. Everything is set up for the coaches and players. You can have a camera going while the game is going on to get wide shots. You can actually be breaking down the film while the game is going on.

Once you send us the film, we break it down for you. Coaches can edit the data. If you want four different editions of the offense for each coach, we can have that broken down the way you request the breakdowns. Then, you can share this with the players. We can make cut-ups online. We can do a lot of other things with the program. You can pause in the film, and you can mark on the film anywhere you want just with the mouse. The coach can type notes on top of the machine if he wants to add something. The player will know what he is looking for by having the coach mark on the computer that will be on the DVD when the players look at the DVD.

This system is great for practice film. You can make corrections for players. We had coaches in Texas, Nebraska, and Kansas use the program this past season. Since the fall of 2008, we have had over 130 high schools and small colleges sign up to use our system since that time.

Once you get the system set up on your computer, you can do reports like formation reports and many other useful reports that will help you later in the season. We have all of the stats set where you can pull them up at anytime. You can pull up special clips of an opponent's plays. You can place them at the bottom of the computer and view those clips one at a time.

Another feature is the fact that the program handles all of your intercutting for you. Once we get the film uploaded, you can view it from a lot of different locations via the pre-set codes on the program.

If you are using a different company to break down your film, you can send that copy to Hudl and we can start making a highlight film for you. Instead of the coaches having to dig out the film and select the highlights, we can do all of that for you. All the coaches have to do is to push the star button on the computer, and it can be saved as a highlight clip. This highlight tape can be sent to parents, college recruiters, or to the players. Those individuals can order a DVD online. This helps the coaches and saves them a lot of time and effort.

The points I have covered are a few of the things Hudl can do to save the coach time and make the game film available a lot quicker. The $800 covers one sport. Hudl is a multiple sport program. Schools can get both football and basketball for $1200, and that covers both boys and girls basketball. For $1600, all of the sports in a school can be included in the program. We have football, boys and girls basketball, wrestling, softball, track and field, and baseball on our programs. This is one benefit several schools are enjoying by having all sports covered on the program.

I want to have Coach Mike Bloomgren of the New York Jets come up and tell us how the Jets used the program the last two years. I will tell you that the Cleveland Browns started using our program last year as well. I am going to turn it over to Mike.

Coach Mike Bloomgren: New York Jets

I am going to talk about Hudl Pro. It is the first product these people developed. I am going to briefly tell you how we used it.

The first thing we did with the program was with our rookies. The moment the rookies were drafted, we got them on the phone with the Hudl people. Instantly, they had our playbook, our cut-ups, and the install plays we were going to use for the rookie camp we were going to have the next weekend. It was a big deal for us because of the number of new players we had to work with. What I am telling you, all of our new players had all of our playbook, all of the cut-ups and formations, and all of the information they would need for the camp the next week. They had the information by Sunday night after the draft on Saturday and Sunday. Therefore, when they came to camp on Thursday, there was no surprise for them. They could actually speak our language. We could speak to them about our system without introducing new information to them.

Another thing we thought was good about Hudl was the fact that all of the DVD cut-ups you can access from a remote place. All you need is a high-speed internet connection. We get our players online and ask them to look at certain cut-ups. As coaches, we know we do not sleep a lot at certain times. If you wake up in the middle of the night and want to watch a certain cut-up, it is available. You can make a note about practice and send it out right away.

If you want to make a note to one of the players on the practice film, I hit *send* then *check text message* and it hits their phone that they have in their hand. They always have their phone with them. It tells them I have sent them a couple of clips to view on the system. I can draw on the film or I can do what I want to do on those film clips. Those clips will be on Hudl as soon as they open it up.

Another great advantage from a coach's standpoint is the fact we do not have to go into the office Sunday nights after the game. We do whatever we do in the parking lot, and I go home and I grade the film from home. The Hudl has our film up on the system before I make it home after the game. I sit there with my Cowboy Remote® or you can use an Xbox® remote. The Xbox is unbelievable how you can load the film. This is a real value for the coaching staff. As all coaches are trying to balance our family life, and in getting your work done, it is a real asset for coaches.

Another thing about Hudl was this presentation. That is what sold us on the Hudl initially. You can do a PowerPoint® presentation; you can stick them into Hudl and they are ready to view. You can integrate them with video or show it any way you want it. You can have a PowerPoint slide or a video slide. You can have a video slide and a PowerPoint slide. You do not have to worry about switching between them. You can have notations all over the video and film. I am not sure if they showed your session where you can spot-shadow. You can spot-shadow the safety coming down in the box. It is an unbelievable tool. I think it is the biggest technique that has hit our game since the 1990s. Anywhere your players have an Internet connection, they can get on Hudl. It is a tremendous tool for helping the rookies get ahead of the game.

Coach Alexander

That does it for tonight except for the pizza. Let's give a big round of applause for the college speakers and for the Hudl group for their information and for the pizza.

ABOUT THE AUTHOR

Paul Alexander is entering his 16th season on the Bengals coaching staff. It's his 15th straight season as offensive line coach, and since the hiring of Marvin Lewis as Bengals head coach in 2003, Alexander has had the added role of assistant head coach.

As line coach, Alexander has molded a unit that has helped make the Bengals one of the NFL's most respected offenses in recent years. Last season, the line weathered a tougher-than-usual campaign in the injury department and still led the offense to a number of noteworthy league and franchise achievements.

As a unit, the offense ranked eighth in the NFL in net yards (341.4 per game) and sixth in passing yards

(239.6). The team ranked eighth in the league in scoring. The line aided individual accomplishments that included a club-record 4035 passing yards for Carson Palmer, an NFL-leading 1369 receiving yards for wide receiver Chad Ochocinco, and 1309 rushing yards for running back Rudi Johnson. Over the last three seasons, the line has paved the way for 4221 yards and 36 rushing touchdowns for Rudi Johnson, the most ever in each category by a Bengal in any three-year span.

All of the previous stats were produced despite injuries that sidelined starting center Rich Braham for 14 games, starting left tackle Levi Jones for 10 games, and starting right guard Bobbie Williams for three contests. Alexander coached excellent replacement performances by second-year center Eric Ghiaciuc, rookie tackle Andrew Whitworth, and third-year guard Stacy Andrews. Meanwhile, Alexander continued his guidance of the career of tackle Willie Anderson, who was named in 2006 to his fourth consecutive Pro Bowl, three of those as an AFC starter.

In 2005, Alexander directed a unit primarily responsible for the best pass protection in franchise history. The 2005 club set franchise records for the fewest total sacks allowed (21) and sacks allowed per game (1.3).

On Oct. 22, 2000, Alexander's Bengals line shared the glory of a 278-yard rushing game by running back Corey Dillon versus Denver. It was an NFL record at the time, and it still stands second in league annals entering the 2007 season. The Bengals' 407 total rushing yards in that game ranks as the fifth-highest single-game total in NFL history, and as the most yards in 56 years. The last team to top it was the New York Giants, who gained 423 against Baltimore in 1950.

Alexander began his NFL coaching career in 1992 as tight ends coach of the New York Jets under head coach Bruce Coslet. When Coslet moved to Cincinnati as offensive coordinator in 1994, Alexander joined him in the role of Bengals' tight ends coach. But Alexander's first love in football was always the offensive line. He was afforded the chance to take over that job for the Bengals in 1995 and has held it ever since.

Alexander is a product of distinguished teachers. He coached under Joe Paterno at Penn State and Bo Schembechler at Michigan. He also was offensive line coach at Central Michigan, a school whose coach, Herb Deromedi, ranks with Paterno and Schembechler among the winningest coaches in NCAA Division I history.

He's a native of Rochester, New York, where he attended Cardinal Mooney High School. He was an Academic All-American at Cortland State (NY) and holds a master's degree in exercise physiology from Penn State.

ALEXANDER AT A GLANCE

- 2003-present: Cincinnati Bengals, Assistant Head Coach/Offensive Line Coach
- 1994-2002: Cincinnati Bengals, Offensive Line Coach
- 1992-1993: New York Jets, Offensive Line Coach
- 1987-1991: Central Michigan University, Offensive Line Coach
- 1985-1986: University of Michigan, Graduate Assistant
- 1982-1984: Penn State University, Graduate Assistant

GOAL-LINE RUNNING PLAYS

University of Maryland

Good evening. It is a pleasure to be here. I have tapes that go back in time when this clinic first started. This clinic has grown into the premier clinic in the country.

Being an offensive line coach, you want to keep an edge. The game is constantly evolving. The people that have developed this clinic have been my mentors through the years. I have coached in high school. I have gone through all of those lift-a-thons, and I have taped the ankles. I coached eight years in high school. Then, I was fortunate to get a job at the College of William & Mary. From there, I went to Northwestern, Stanford, and, now, Maryland.

When Paul called me to speak, I asked him what topic I should lecture on. I told him I had been to the clinic several times, and I had heard a lot of different topics discussed at the clinic. I picked a topic that has not been discussed that much, so I agreed to do my deal and talk on goal-line offense. Here are the plays we are going to talk about tonight.

GOAL-LINE RUN PLAYS

- 34/35 zone
- 36/37 chip
- 16/17 power gl
- 38/39 load option
- 36/37 grace

You can see it is going to be a difficult task in that I have five running plays to cover in 30 minutes. I want to show the plays on the overhead, and then I want to show you films of the plays in game action.

Our head coach is the type of coach that wants to run the ball downhill. He wants to run over the defense with the power blocking. Make no mistake about it, we are going to run the football. We are

going to run the fullback in the game. That may be alien to those of you who run the shotgun offense and the spread offense. There is nothing wrong with running that offense. It is like Baskin Robbins® in that they have 31 flavors. You do whatever it takes to get it done. We are a two-back offense with 21 and 22 personnel.

Here are our goal-line thoughts. Nothing is more disheartening than to drive the ball down the field and not "cash it in." We have all been there. You end up with turnovers, and the defense makes the plays, and you waste an opportunity. Therefore, we stress these points to get it done.

- Finish the deal.
- Do what you do.
- Practice effectively.
- Average one yard a play.
- Maintain consistency.

FINISH THE DEAL

You must convince your kids to get it in. Field goals are nice, but that is not the deal. The goal is to put the ball in the end zone. You preach to them to be tough and you work on techniques, which is all good; but you must switch gears on the goal line. You must give a little more from the heart—an extra effort to get the ball into the end zone.

DO WHAT YOU DO

If running off-tackle got you down to the goal line, then keep running the off-tackle play. Don't change horses when you get down there. Do what you have been doing to get you to the goal line or red zone.

If you are a spread team, run the spread on the goal line. That is what you know, so run the spread offense. Obviously, you have some short-yardage plays in that offense. The wishbone is good, but don't just change to be changing the offense without good reason on the goal line.

PRACTICE EFFECTIVELY

Last year, we had 800 snaps. We had 21 goal-line plays. All offensive line coaches have a desire to practice to the point where your kids do not make mistakes, and we want to go over and over the goal-line offense. That is all well and good. However, you must do some other things correctly to be successful.

We used to carry four running plays and a pass play in our goal-line offense. We are going to change the formations, but the thing we stress is to practice effectively. We practice on Tuesday. We introduce the plays, and we walk through the plays against the defense. Then, we will go semi-live against a scout team. We practice again on Thursday, and then we walk through the four plays we are going to use again on Saturday morning.

Goal-line scrimmage with contact against the defense is the first thing we do in spring practice. We like that mind-set of getting the offense to think about getting the ball into the end zone. This way, the players are not going against each other at long distances.

AVERAGE ONE YARD PER PLAY

We go into this offense at the four-yard line. If we can get one yard per play, that means we are staying on track.

MAINTAIN CONSISTENCY

The last three seasons we have been very successful. We have averaged over 90 percent consistency on the goal line in the last three years.

At the University of Maryland, we break everything down in our offense, and I am responsible for the goal-line offense. I start with breaking down the films. These are the things I am looking for against an opponent.

GOAL-LINE SCOUTING

The first thing I want to know is this: What is your base goal-line defense? I am going to check the early tapes to see if you changed your offense on the goal line or if you ran the same base offense.

The next point I want to know is this: What do you run on defense? Do you run the 6-2, gap 8, the seven-diamond defense, or their defenses? If you are in the open defense, do you run a lot of blitzes? When you go to the goal line, do you match up with your personnel? If we go with our 21 personnel on the goal line, what will you be in defensively? I want to know who will be the substitutes. That would dictate our substitutes pattern and what we do there. Whom do you substitute for on the goal line and whom do you take out? Do you bring in another corner or do you bring in a big guy? Do you bring in an extra linebacker? What is your substitute process? We keep a sheet in the press box so we know right away if goal-line personnel is coming into the game.

We want to know if we can read the slant angles. We want to know if the 5 technique moved inside to a 4 technique because they slant a lot on defense. We want to know if the 2i technique is going to move to a 2 technique because he is always looping outside. We want to know if the linebackers are up tight so we can see when the double-blitz-stunt-up-the-middle is coming. You look at the tape, and you are teaching the coaching points to your goal-line offense. We tell our offense they are responsible to know the details about the goal-line defense. However, it is our job as coaches to present the defensive information to them.

We want to know when the defense runs goal-line blitzes, if we can tell the base coverage. We want to know who has the tight end. We feel that is a big deal down on the goal line. We know most of the time he is open if we have to throw the football.

We want to know who covers the quarterback naked. We want to know which defensive line plays high because that is who we are going to attack.

The first play we are going to run is a glorified lead play. For us, it is our *34* or *35 zone play*. We are going to run against one of two fronts. We call this a *zone front* (Diagram #1). We are going to read the tackle's block. We are in a four-point stance. We are crowding the football, and we are butts and elbows on the line.

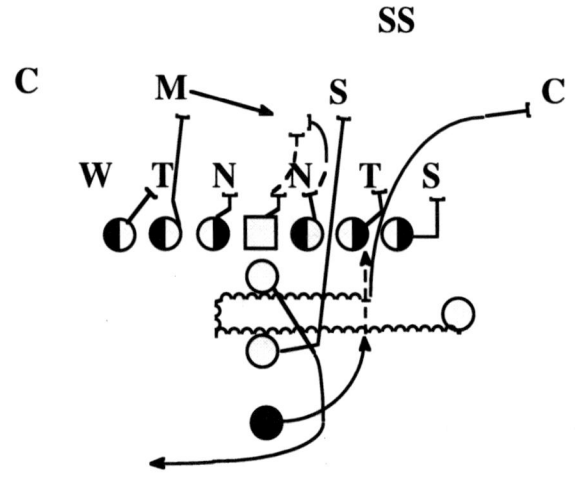

Diagram #1. Lead Play, 34/35 Zone

We want the helmet of the offensive line about six inches off the ground. In my opinion, it is a game of leverage down on the goal line. We can go from a two-point stance, four-point stance, or a six-point stance on the goal line. We are crowding the ball up front.

The fullback is at four yards deep, and the tailback is at six yards deep. The quarterback opens up to the playside, and exchanges the ball as quickly as he can to the tailback. We run our naked out of this play. The tailback is going to read the block by the strongside tackle.

Landmarks are huge. Our head coach grew up as an offensive line coach; he likes to check us on our techniques, and he wants to know what we are doing. He is an offensive line coach at heart.

We like to run the play toward the wing set, but we can run the play away from the wing set. We use different types of motion with this play.

We read the block by the tackle. The tackle is down-the-middle landmark. We do not want to deviate from that. If the defensive tackle goes outside, we take him outside. He takes the man the way he wants to go, and the back must read his block. I cannot give you all of the looks we see on defense, but we can have the Z-back block a little differently on the play. He could swap blocks with the tight end and block the Sam end. We see this defense against our base set offense.

We feel we will get a good double-team block with the center and onside guard. If we can, we want the center to come off the block and pick up the linebacker coming across to make the play. The offside guard checks the A gap and blocks the 2i technique. The fullback is reading the tackle's block. The tailback is reading the block by the tackle as well. We do roll block on the backside. We want our backside linemen to get their hats across the knees of the defenders and then we want them to get their heads across the defenders. Swapping does not get it done down on the goal line. You must get *push* down on the goal line. That is a big push for us.

On the backside, we are C blocking this play. We are blocking Will over the top. We also have the Mike linebacker on the run to the play.

The defense is tight, and we expect the out stunt on the backside. We expect the inside down men to come outside and the linebackers to come to fill the A gaps on the play.

We can make a call on the backside and bring the tackle down inside. In addition, we can zone block the backside.

We see the 5-3 stack defense a lot of times. I do not like this play against this stack. I like it a lot better against the 6-2 defense. We know we must be ready to block the 5-3 stack look (Diagram #2). We are reading the first down lineman. It is a big block for the inside end. He must get leverage against the defender.

We zigzag motion across and back as we did before. We can change the blocking if we see the end and corner playing games. Against the defensive tackle, we can run a deuce block with the double-team on the tackle, and have the end coming off the bump block, to pick up the middle linebacker. If the Mike runs underneath the block, the center has him on the over block.

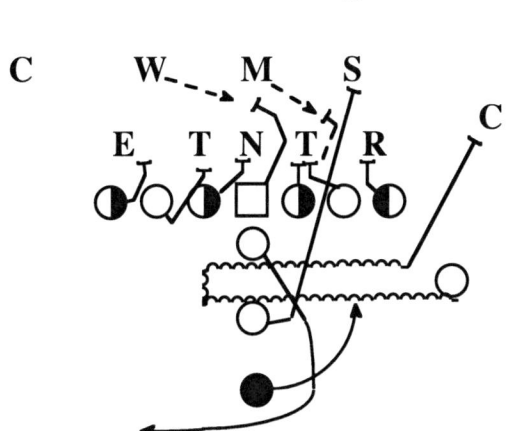

Diagram #2. 34/35 Zone vs. 5-3 Stack

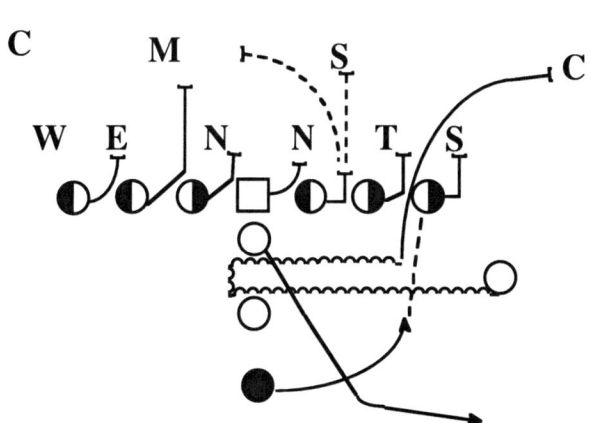

Diagram #3. 36/37 Chip vs. 6-2 Defense

We are three-way zoning on the backside. The backside guard, tackle, and end have the defensive nose, tackle, and end. We come off the nose man and climb to the Will backer. We get the Mike on the run-through underneath. If the end is coming inside and the corner is coming off the edge, we can bump the tackle and end to pick up the backside rush.

Now, we take the play out one play wider. We run *36/37 chip* against the 5-3 stack (Diagram #3). It is the same play, but now we are reading the block by the tight end—our landmarks change. Now, we have outside landmarks for the onside line blocks. If the inside man goes inside, we are going to zone scheme. The onside guard is going to step flat, gain some ground, and check the veer and check the backer. The center is going to help on the onside down lineman. That is not a hard block because it is only a six-inch step for the center.

We call the block by the strong guard a three-prong tackle. He may assist with the tackle, climb block on the Sam linebacker, or slide over to pick up the Mike linebacker. The fullback and tailback are reading the block by the tight end now. If the Sam is outside wide, we look for the corner to be inside.

This is where I like this play against this look. The chip is what we call the block on the 7 technique. We get a great double-team block on the 7 technique. We want to knock him off the ball. We want push at the point of attack. It is a lateral zone play. We are rocking that 7 technique back on the

play. At the same time, we are aware of the run-through by the Sam linebacker, and we are working up to the Mike linebacker on the backside.

If we have a hard time blocking the 3 technique with the guard, we can single block on the Sam backer, and have the tackle come down and chip block on the 3 technique. The guard or tackle can come off on the Mike linebacker.

Next, I want to look at our *16/17 power goal-line* play (Diagram #4). This may be one of our best plays on the goal line. It is a good play against the 5-3 stack look.

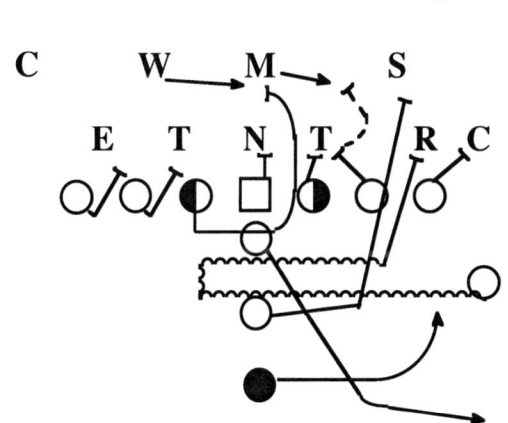

Diagram #4. 16/17 Power Goal-Line Play

We like to run this when we have to block the end outside. Most of the time, we see man coverage. The tight end must be able to block the

R defender. Most teams try to cover the tight end with the R defender. We try to use that to our advantage. Rather than having the tight end blocking down on the 7 technique and holding that block all day, we are going to block him out on the corner. By the scouting report, we can usually tell what the R defender is playing, man or zone, by his stance. He is either going to play the end man-to-man or he is coming on the rush.

Against the 6-2 defense, we trey block with the onside tackle and end. We are in an all gap-control set. We are blocking back to the Mike linebacker. If we see the blitz coming down the Mike backer, we can move the double-team block down to the guard and have one of them pick up Mike off the trey block. We end up with the tight end solo on the 5 technique.

Away from the wing, we run the option play to the backside (Diagram #5). We can run a glorified G play. It is the same blocking as the chip blocking. We call the play *38/39 lead option*. We get a double-team chip block with the end and tackle. One of the two will come off and pick up the Mike linebacker.

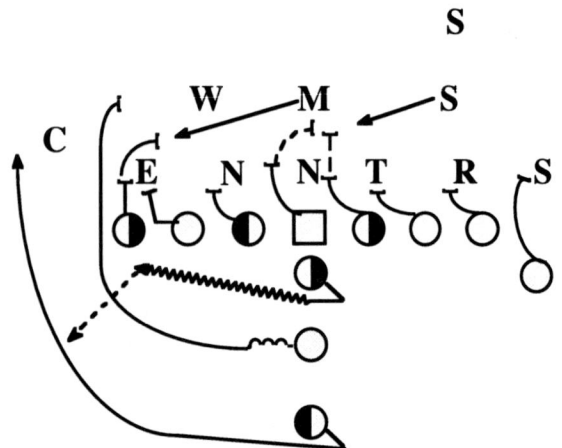

Diagram #5. 38/39 Load Option

We can put the fullback in soft motion, or he can take three parallel steps. He is going to read the end man on the line of scrimmage and read his path to determine if he is going to block the Mike linebacker.

The quarterback lifts his backside foot, pivots his foot, turns, and runs down the line of scrimmage and attacks the end man on the line of scrimmage.

We get a 4x4 blocking scheme on the corner. It has been a good play for us over the years.

Next, we look at *38/39 load option* against the 6-2 alignment. Depending on the alignment at the point of attack, we can rub-trade against the tackle and Mike linebacker (Diagram #6). The tight end kisses soft on the tackles and comes off on the Mike linebacker. We have the guard step at the 2i and climb to the linebacker. The center is on the 2i defender.

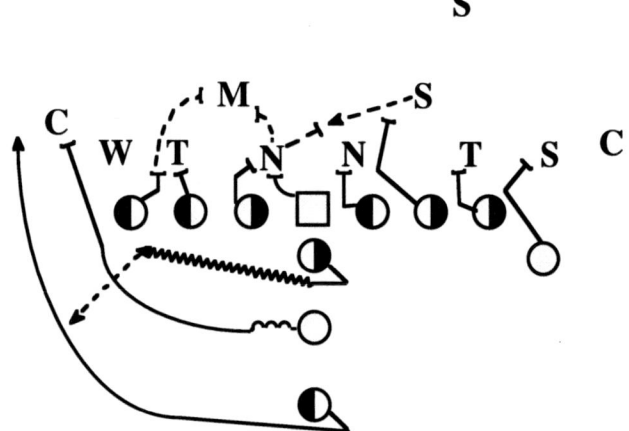

Diagram #6. 38/39 Load Option vs. 6-2 Defense

We are going to option off the Will linebacker. The fullback is blocking the corner. Everything happens quick at the goal line. The quarterback must be ready to pitch the ball right away.

Our next play is the *LD 36/37 grace*. We put the wing to the opposite and go tackle over. Then, we run a G play out of this set (Diagram #7). This play has been really good to us because everyone thinks the tight end and Z-back are on the left side. They rarely see the tackle over.

The call in the huddle would be, "Scream to whatever." That tells the left tackle that he is going to line up on the opposite side with the other tackle. All we are doing is blocking old-fashioned wing-T offense. It is gap down, backer onside. I am showing my roots here. I am an old Tubby Raymond, Delaware wing-T guy from way back. All you are doing is blocking down on this play.

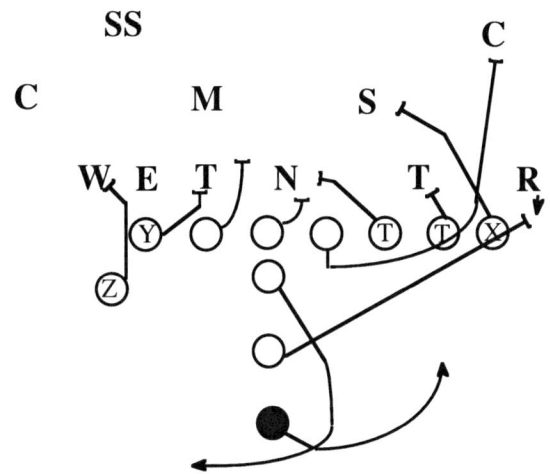

**Diagram #7. I Left Over 36/37
Grace vs. 6-2 Unadjusted**

The fullback has to kick out. The pulling guard has to check to block up the alley. It is hard to tell what the defense is going to be playing against this set. It is hard to script the offense when you do not know what the defense is going to be playing.

Against the 5-3 stack, we pull the onside guard and turn him up in the gap through to the first man to show past the line of scrimmage (Diagram #8). The X end seals inside on the Sam linebacker. We have good blocking angles inside on the strongside. The fullback blocks the R backer outside.

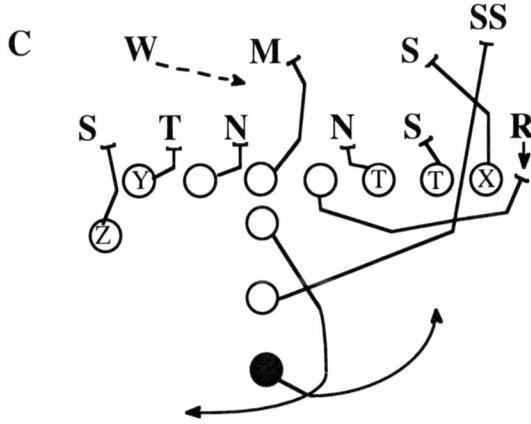

**Diagram #8. I Left, Tite Over
36 Grace vs. 5-3 Stack**

I know I am talking fast, and I want to go to some film now to show you drills we use in teaching these plays. This will be the same format in that we will be running the zone and the chip plays.

GOAL-LINE BLOCKING DRILLS

This is how we practice the offense. I do not want to step on the toes of the vendors. We get those big stand-up dummies and turn them on their sides. They weigh about 90 pounds each. The defender holds the top part of the dummies on the edge with the handles. We are going to drive the dummies for 10 yards. We are going to drive the dummies low. You cannot do this drill on a level sled. You cannot get down that low on the sled. We cannot go live every day in practice. We line them up, left side to right side, and we block.

We actually crawl and block in the drill as we go down the field. The drill really becomes ugly, but I really do not care. After we drive the dummies far enough, we turn around and come back the other side doing the crawling. We want the blocker down low with his weight on his hands and knees. He must bend his elbows. We want him to drive the shields with his shoulders down low and his butt up high in the air.

The next drill we work on is the *backside cut-off drill*. We line our offensive linemen up in a four-point stance. It is different because the weight is different. The linemen must practice this technique. If we ask that backside tackle to cut off a 3 technique, it is difficult in a four-point stance. He must practice doing this technique from a four-point stance (It is easier from a three-point stance). We drop the inside foot, and we move the backside shoulder on the playside kneecap. They must practice this from a four-point stance if they expect to do well on the goal line.

I have some film of the zone play that I want to show down on the goal line. We are in 32 personnel. We are in a four-point stance, and we are coming off the ball low. We run big on big and knock the defense off the line of scrimmage. We are still reading the block by the playside tackle. When we get inside the four-yard line, we only take a six-inch split. We pack in tight, and we are going to knock you off the ball.

If we call *chip*, it means we are going outside. We read the block by the tight end. We motion the wingback on his zigzag motion. We are going outside on the chip play.

To finish up, I want to show you the goal-line plays in the order in which we covered them.

How many high school coaches do we have here? I see quite a few. My hat's off to the high school coaches here today. As college coaches, we kind of inherit your work. You do all of the grunt work. In this day and age, you have an awesome responsibility. It used to be, back in 1980, when college coaches made home visits to players they wanted to recruit to their college, they usually had two parents in the family. Today, you need a scorecard to keep up with the families anymore.

As a high school coach, you have become more of a male figure—more important than you ever dreamed possible. My hat is off to you for taking time to become a better coach and a better person. College and pro coaches inherit your efforts. Men, it has been a pleasure. Come to see us anytime. Take care.

ABOUT THE AUTHOR

After coaching in the Big Ten and Pac-10, Tom Brittan has found a home with Maryland in the Atlantic Coast Conference. The veteran coach is in his ninth season as the Terrapins' offensive line coach. He boasts more than 35 years of coaching experience, including 26 at the collegiate level.

The Maryland offensive line has been one of the team's strengths since 2001, producing six first team All-Atlantic Coast Conference performers and a handful of other players honored by both the league and national media. In 2007, Andrew Crummey was tabbed a second-team All-American, while Scott Burley earned all-conference honors.

Prior to coming to Maryland, Brattan spent two years (1999 to 2000) at Stanford University, where he served as the Cardinals' line coach in charge of centers and guards. Stanford went 8-4 in 1999 and had wins over Arizona, UCLA, Oregon State, and Notre Dame on the way to a Rose Bowl bid. The 1999 Stanford offense scored at least 31 points in all but three games and hit the 50-point plateau three times. That year, Brattan's offensive line allowed just 15 sacks despite 385 passing attempts (one sack for every 27 attempts).

Brattan took his first full-time job at the collegiate level at William & Mary in 1983 as an offensive backfield coach. After just one season, he was promoted to offensive coordinator and served the remainder of his tenure (1984 to 1991) in that capacity. He also worked with the offensive line at William & Mary. In that time, the Tribe advanced to the NCAA Division I-AA playoffs on three occasions. From 1986 to 1990, William & Mary earned national rankings in three seasons (number 9 in 1986; number 13 in 1989; number 7 in 1990). The success was largely a product of Brattan's offensive design as his unit ranked in the top 20 in offense in 1985 and 1986, while it had the top-rated attack in Division I-AA for the 1990 season and the sixth best in 1991.

Brattan took his success at the I-AA level to his next job, Northwestern, where he resided from 1992 to 1998 as the offensive line coach. In Brattan's first three years at the school, the Wildcats continued to struggle, pushing their streak of seasons without a winning mark to 23.

Then, in 1995, the Wildcats were in the national spotlight as they came seemingly out of nowhere to win the Big Ten championship for the first time in 47 years and advanced to the Rose Bowl where they ultimately fell to Southern California. They finished that season—despite the Rose Bowl loss—ranked seventh in the nation with a 10-2 record. Brattan's offensive line allowed just eight sacks all year while helping propel Darnell Autry to a new school rushing record. Northwestern finished fifth nationally in rushing. The Wildcats went on to post a combined 15-1 conference record in 1995 and 1996, taking the Big Ten crown both years after having won just five league games in the previous three years. In 1996, they earned a bid to play Tennessee in the Citrus Bowl.

Brattan got his start in coaching as a graduate assistant at his alma mater, Delaware, in 1972. After one year in Newark, he took his first full-time coaching post at Highland Springs (Va.) High School as an offensive line coach. After three years (1973 to 1975) at Highland Springs, he moved back to his home state and took his first head coaching job at

McKean High School in 1977. He spent one year at McKean—the same high school that helped produce Maryland legend Randy White—before moving back to Virginia and taking over as the head coach at Lloyd C. Bird High School. After serving at Bird in 1978, he returned to Highland Springs—this time as a head coach—for his final four years (1979 to 1982) at the prep level.

A native of Newark, Delaware, Brattan is a 1972 graduate of his hometown school where he earned his bachelor's degree in history and later earned his master's degree in education in 1977. He was a member of the Blue Hen football team and earned a varsity letter in 1971. He and his wife, Anne, have three children—Kristen, Kate, and Megan, a current Maryland student.

BRATTAN AT A GLANCE

- 2001-present: University of Maryland, Offensive Line Coach
- 1999-2000: Stanford University, Offensive Line Coach
- 1992-1998: Northwestern University, Offensive Line Coach
- 1984-1991: William & Mary, Offensive Coordinator/Offensive Line Coach
- 1983: William & Mary, Offensive Backfield
- 1979-1982: Highland Springs High School (Va.), Head Football Coach
- 1978: Lloyd C. Bird High School (Va.), Head Football Coach
- 1977: MacKean High School (De.), Head Football Coach
- 1973-1975: Highland Springs High School (Va.), Offensive Line Coach
- 1972: Delaware, Graduate Assistant

ONE- AND TWO-BACK POWER PLAYS

University of Connecticut

Thank you for the introduction, Paul. We ran the power play this year because we had a great tailback in Donald Brown. He did a great job for us, and he was drafted in the first round. Donald Brown did a great job for us.

I want to jump into the one- and two-back power play that Donald Brown ran so well for us. The thing I like about our power play is the fact that we can use the same blocking schemes and techniques that we use on other plays. In addition, we have a gap play that we can run that is similar to the power play. It is like the zone plays in that you can run them inside or outside. The thing I like about the power play is that it is a very versatile play from the one-back or the two-back set.

It is also a physical play. It is a play that we are looking for a double-team block on the frontside, or a combo block working up to a linebacker. And, we are bringing a pulling guard to the frontside. We are getting people to help us on the frontside. It is also a mentality play for our players. We have been able to run the football well with this play.

Whenever we struggle offensively, our offensive linemen will say, "Coach, run the power play." They believe in what they are doing. That is the way it is for a lot of things you do in football. It is what your kids believe. It does not matter how you coach it or anything else, it is what your kids believe. I have sat up front here and learned a lot of things from the speakers at this clinic. It is a pleasure to be here to share a few ideas with you on the things we do. There are a lot of ways to skin a cat, and I am going to talk about the things we have been successful with in our program.

For us, the play is an inside-gap play. That is the mentality for us on the play. The only time the tight end is not involved in the gap is when the tackle is uncovered. He is going to base block and go from there. Other than that situation, it is an inside-gap play.

If the inside adjacent lineman is uncovered, it becomes a combo. We have the guard and tackle working together in what we call a *deuce* block. If the tackle and tight end are working together, you will hear me saying it is a *trey* block. That is a key block for us. The way we teach the block is to take an inside lateral step, with the second step up the field. If we are running a deuce block, the tackle is also taking an inside lateral step. We want to get cheek to cheek and take the 3-technique defender off the ball.

The difference between the deuce block and the trey block is for the tight end. The tight end will use the first step as a lateral step, but he is going to work on making contact on the hip of the defender. We want to get both horizontal and vertical movement with the tight end involved. This is the reason we have the tight end work the hip. We feel we can get a little more push with the end blocking on the hip. We do that one thing different with the tight end.

2008 POWER PLAY TOTALS

- 193 attempts
- 1,274 yards gained
- 6.6 yards per attempt

2008 TWO-BACK POWER TOTALS

- 110 attempts
- 682 yards gained
- 6.2 yards per attempt

The reason I say the play is versatile is because it is a scheme you can use with two tight ends, but also with a split end set. This is against a 4-4 defense with the two linebackers stacked in the middle. The center is blocking back against the backside gap man (Diagram #1). We want to block the 2i with the onside guard. The tackle is going to check the 2i and pick up the near linebacker.

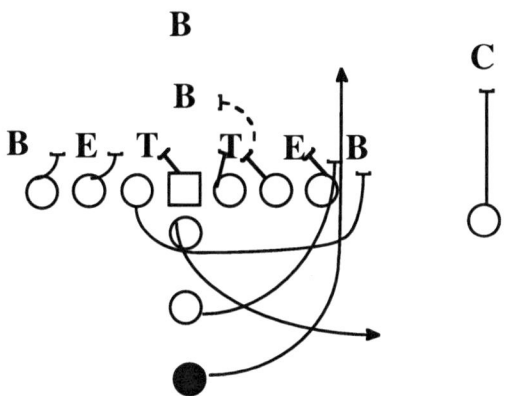

Diagram #1. Vs. 4-4 Stack Alignment

We want to make a trey block on the 5 technique. The tackle will work to the near linebacker. The onside guard will take the gap defender alone. The fullback gets on what we call a *banana course*. His deal is to trap the heels of the tackle. He is going to go off the heels of the tackle and hit the first defender that shows up.

The backside guard will make what we call a *square pull*. Some teams use a skip-pull where they step with the backside foot, staying square with the shoulders. We take a square pull where we step with the inside foot. Most of the time, we do not want the guard to get his shoulders at more than a 45-degree angle. The reason we take that angle is because we want to blow up anything that is coming off the edge. The backside tackle and end are on a slide-hinge block.

The effort on the backside is very important. They need to stay involved in the play and maintain their blocks until the ball is past them.

The onside end is responsible for the linebacker on his side. In some cases, the linebacker is picked off by the double-team block, and he is free to continue downfield to pick up the secondary defender.

We do not want the onside tackle coming off the ball on the down block too quickly. What I tell those down linemen on the deuce and trey blocks is this: I want them to block the down man first and to see the linebacker next. If we can, we want the tackle to push the defensive lineman into the linebacker. We are committed to blocking that down man first.

On the deuce block for the onside guard, we want his shoulders to remain square to the line of scrimmage. He can turn them slightly inside, but we want to make sure he is parallel to the line of scrimmage on the deuce block.

If the tackle is uncovered, the tight end will take a lateral step inside against an inside technique or a head-up technique. If the defense covers the tackle, we want to get him covered, and if we can "know" him off the line, that is great.

We look for the defense to blitz the linebacker through the B gap against the deuce block. The guard can pick up the blitz to the A gap, and the tackle must pick up the blitz to the B gap. The pulling guard will switch assignments, and he will end up blocking the backside linebacker.

We can run the play from our 21 personnel. This is the play back to the tight end side (Diagram #2). The end takes the down man on his outside. The tackle runs the deuce block with the guard on the tackle and linebacker. The fullback runs his banana route and picks up the first man on the edge. The pulling guard takes the first opposite-color jersey to show on the edge. The block of the tight end is very important on this play. We want the pulling guard to be more aggressive. We do not want him to guess who he is going to block. We tell him, "When in doubt, block up in the hole."

Our next look is against the 4-3 defense. The fullback picks up the Sam linebacker (Diagram #3). The pulling guard picks up the Mike linebacker.

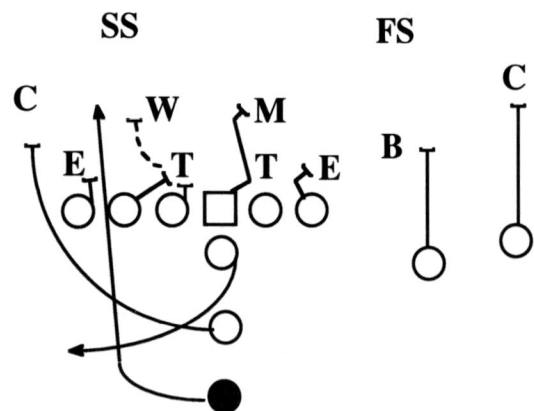

Diagram #2. Power to Split End

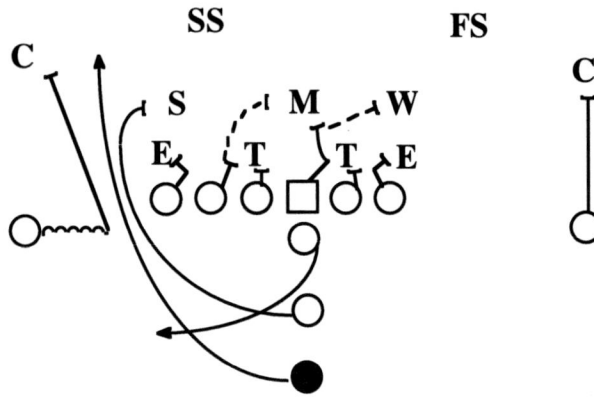

Diagram #3. Power vs. 4-3 Defense

We can move the fullback from an outside position and motion him back inside to his fullback spot. It gives the play a different look to the defense. We can trade tight ends on the formation as well.

We do run the power play to the split end side. A lot of it has to do with the match-up we have. If we have the right match-up, we will go ahead and run the power play. We just need the looks that we like to run the play to the split end side. A lot of it depends on whether our fullback can match up with the defensive end.

2008 ONE-BACK POWER TOTALS

- 81 attempts
- 555 yards
- 6.9 yards per attempt

Next, I want to show you some of our one-back plays. Now, it is the same play except the tight end is taking the place of the fullback (Diagram #4). We would need one less defender in the box on this alignment. We see a lot of 4-2 looks, or a 40-nickel type of look. If the defense has seven in the box, we are going to check out of the play.

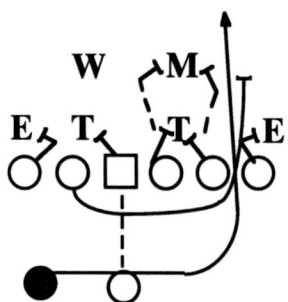

Diagram #4. One-Back Power Play

Against a zone blitz, we can make an adjustment with the front blockers and make it an A-gap play. The defense is coming off the backside, and we need to run away from the blitz. The defense slants the front line toward the shortside. We block our onside guard on the down lineman to stop the slant (Diagram #5). The guard knows that we are going to run the play in the A gap. The guard pulls and leads the play through the A gap and blocks the linebacker.

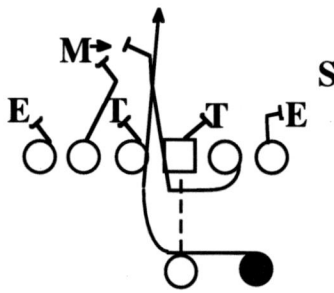

Diagram #5. One-Back Power vs. Blitz

I want to go over something we changed up this year. When you are in a one-back set, you ask the question, "What are we going to do?" We may say we are going to "base up" and block our basic alignment for the play. Normally, against the Okie look or the 50 look, this is how we blocked for the one-back power (Diagram #6). We ended up with two single blocks with the tackle and end.

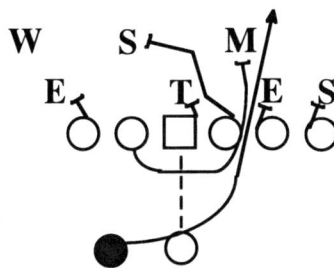

Diagram #6. Two Single Blocks

We made this change last year. We combo blocked the tackle and Mike linebacker (Diagram #7). We pulled the backside guard, and instead of him going up in the hole after the Mike linebacker, he came outside and blocked on the end outside. It was a big play for us last year. On the playside we pulled the guard and blocked outside on the outside man at the point of attack. On the backside, we blocked the tackle on the defensive end. In one game, the tailback ran for 260 yards, and a lot of those yards came on this play.

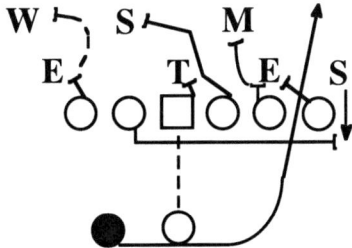

Diagram #7. Change-Up Blocking

It has been a great pleasure for me to be here. If you have questions, feel free to give me a call. Head Coach Randy Edsall is very receptive to having coaches come in to visit. We are willing to share with you what we do in this game. It was a great pleasure to be here today. Thank you.

ABOUT THE AUTHOR

A veteran of northeastern football coaching, Mike Foley has just finished his third season as offensive line coach at the University of Connecticut. Prior to Connecticut, Foley completed 21 seasons of involvement with the football team at his alma mater, Colgate University. He had served as the Raiders' offensive coordinator and offensive line coach since 1997.

In his time at Connecticut, Foley has helped bring a collection of young offensive linemen to a group that helped the Huskies to the 2007 Big East title. That group entered the 2008 season with a combined 147 games of playing experience, almost all of them under Foley's guidance.

In 2005, his final year at Colgate, the Raiders posted an 8-4 record and advanced to the NCAA Division I-AA Playoffs. Foley helped coach all seven of Colgate's NCAA playoff squads, including the 2003 team that advanced to the National Championship game. Of the 13 seasons in which Colgate was eligible for the playoffs with Foley aboard, the team qualified seven times. Foley also played a role in each of Colgate's five Patriot League Championship teams (1997, 1999, 2002, 2003, and 2005).

Colgate broke the league record for rushing yardage three times under his tutelage, and led the Patriot League five out of his last nine seasons. During his tenure as offensive coordinator (1997 to 2005), Foley produced 39 All-Patriot League players including 13 on the offensive line. His offensive schemes and the line's blocking helped pave the way for a pair of Walter Payton Award winners, Kenny Gamble in 1987 and Jamaal Branch in 2003.

He began his coaching career as an offensive line coach at Bates College in 1978, before moving the next fall to Dartmouth as the freshman offensive line coach for one season. After one season as offensive line coach at Holy Cross in 1980, he returned to his alma mater as junior varsity head coach and varsity receivers coach. After two seasons in that position, he took over as the offensive line coach in 1983. Foley added the duties of offensive coordinator in 1984.

In 1986, he served as interim head coach during the absence of head coach Fred Dunlap, who was recovering from bypass surgery. Following Dunlap's retirement in 1987, Foley was named head coach of the Raiders, a title he held through 1992, compiling a 21-34 record. He returned to the Hamilton, New York campus in 1997 as offensive coordinator and line coach after three years on the Harvard staff. While with the Crimson, he served as offensive coordinator during his entire stay.

He was a four-year letter winner at Colgate and captain of the 1977 team. A three-year starter at center, he was twice honored as an All-East performer by the Associated Press and, in 1977, was also named to the ECAC All-East squad. In 2004, Foley was inducted into Colgate's Athletic Hall of Honor.

Foley was born in Kittery, Maine, but grew up in Newburyport, Massachusetts. He graduated from Colgate University in 1978 with a degree in economics. Foley and his wife, Kathleen, have two grown children, Erin and Patrick. A football coach like his father, Patrick is the defensive coordinator at the U.S. Merchant Marine Academy.

FOLEY AT A GLANCE

- 2006-present: University of Connecticut, Offensive Line Coach
- 1997-2005: Colgate University, Offensive Coordinator/Offensive Line Coach
- 1993-1997: Harvard University, Offensive Coordinator/Offensive Line Coach
- 1987-1992: Colgate University, Head Football Coach
- 1984-1987: Colgate University, Offensive Coordinator/Offensive Line Coach
- 1983-1984: Colgate University, Offensive Line Coach
- 1981-1983: Colgate University, Junior Varsity Head Coach/Wide Receivers Coach
- 1980-1981: College of Holy Cross, Offensive Line Coach
- 1979-1980: Dartmouth University, Freshman Offensive Line Coach
- 1978-1979: Bates College, Offensive Line Coach

THE SCREEN GAME

Retired NFL Offensive Line Coach

I am glad to be here today. The C.O.O.L. T-shirt that I am wearing, I have had it since 1992. We are the Mushroom Society. When you raise mushrooms, you keep them in the dark and fertilize them with crap. That is the offensive line coach. He is always in the dark watching film, and that is where the name of the society comes from.

In 1977, Bill Walsh became the head coach at Stanford University. He hired me as his line coach. Those of you who have coached at a place like Stanford know the type of athletes you are going to get because of the academics and being in a conference with the University of Southern California. Those two things are not conducive to running the wishbone or veer.

As a line coach, you want to be physical and knock people off the ball. The philosophy at Stanford was the Sid Gillman and Bill Walsh philosophy. That philosophy was: If you run the ball, it is a wasted play. They were going to throw the ball to set up the running game instead of running the ball to set up the passing game. That was a new philosophy for me.

Bill Walsh told me that because of the type of athletes we would get at Stanford, if we run the wishbone or veer, they will get bored. If we run that type of offense, we will lose them. So we are going to throw the ball.

What I am going to show you will pertain to the screen game. When you run the football, the offensive line can be aggressive. However, at Stanford, that was not our mode. Since we were not going to run the ball, we had to be aggressive in our passing game and protection schemes.

Our theory was to create a neutral zone for the offensive line (Diagram #1). The rules say if the earhole of the guard's helmet is on the waistband of the center, the alignment is legal. By aligning on the waistband of the center, we created a neutral zone for the offensive line. The defense could not get their hands on the offensive linemen as quickly as they could if we crowded the ball. The guards and tackles aligned with the earholes on the waistband of the center with a two-foot split between them. If the defense aligned properly, we had created a one-yard neutral zone. We were going to run and pass from that alignment.

Diagram #1. Neutral Zone

We were not going to vary that alignment unless it was a short-yardage or goal-line situation. In short-yardage or goal-line situations, we would crowd the ball. If the defense aligned onside, we had created a neutral zone which allowed us space. When we snapped the ball, the defense was not in the face of the offensive line. The offensive line knew when the ball was going to be snapped, and that allowed us to be aggressive on the first step.

The pocket that we want to create starts six inches outside the offensive tackle. It runs straight back to a point of no return where the pocket bends to the inside (Diagram #2). That is the point of no return. The bend point generally is the third step of the defensive end.

When we snap the ball, the defensive line is not on the offensive line and in their face. We know when the ball is going to be snapped and what the plays will be. That allows the offensive line's first step to be aggressive.

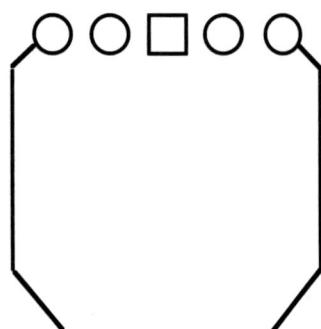

Diagram #2. Passing Pocket

We want to be aggressive in our blocking. In a 65-play game, we do not want to back up 40 times in a pass set and let the defenders attack us. If I am a guard and the defender is head-up, the most dangerous thing he can do is go inside of the guard. The first thought of the offensive guard is to protect the inside. On the snap of the ball, the guard steps into the neutral zone and meets the defender in that zone. He steps with his inside foot and brings up his second step as quickly as he can for balance. He meets the defender in the neutral zone.

Every day in practice we go 1-on-1 with the defensive line. The thing the defender hates the most is the short set because it takes away their first move. If the offensive lineman can take away the defender's first move, he generally does not have a second move.

If the defender is on the outside shade of the guard in a position where he can be reached, the guard takes the same step with the outside foot. He steps to the crotch of the defender with his outside foot and brings up the inside foot for balance. He is aggressively attacking the defender in the neutral zone instead of retreating at the mercy of the defender. We coach all the things in the pass set, but we take on the defender. We have the numbers

as the target in the middle of the defender, and we want the elbows in tight. Those are the fundamental techniques used in pass blocking, but we want to be aggressive and attack the defender.

The line coach is a teacher. There are football coaches, and there are ball coaches. A ball coach is a guy who lined his own field, came up through the ranks, and had to work hard for what he got. Most line coaches are ball coaches. Then, there are the football coaches—those are the media darlings.

The defender will not always align in a tight alignment on the guard. In a passing situation, the defenders like to widen their alignments. The wide 3 technique is almost to the inside eye of the offensive tackle. This presents a problem for the offensive guard. He cannot reach him with his first step. I do not want the offensive lineman to go laterally at any time.

I feel there are only six directions an offensive lineman can move. He can go to the right at a 45-degree angle, to the left at a 45-degree angle, or straight ahead. He can go back to his right at a 45-degree angle, back to his left at a 45-degree angle, or straight back. If the lineman goes in a lateral direction, he creates a natural softness in his set.

The guard cannot reach the defender on his first step. He has to reestablish the line of scrimmage by taking three quick steps to the outside. It is like a dance step. He steps back six inches at a 45-degree angle to the outside with his outside foot. He follows that with a quick inside-foot step to get closer to the defender. He takes the third step and gets aggressive on the defender. The guard is responsible for the depth of the pocket. He wants the quarterback to be able to step up in the pocket and deliver the ball.

That brings me to a short story. When the Cardinals were in St. Louis, we drafted Neil Lomax, who was a run-and-shoot quarterback. Our quarterback was Jimmy Hart, who was a Pro Bowl quarterback. We were playing Seattle in a pre-season game and Lomax came into the game. He took about a 14-step drop and got sacked. After the game, Jim Hanifan, who was the head coach, told me to take Lomax into the offensive linemen meeting and show him the defensive line stunts. I did not know what to tell Lomax. I went to Jimmy Hart and told him what I had to do. I asked him what I should tell Lomax.

He told me if he drops back and hears "Bam, bam, bam," he can stay in the pocket and throw the ball. However, if he hears "Swish, swish, swish," he needs to get out of the pocket and run. That was the All-Pro quarterback, Jim Hart, with a definition of how to avoid the rush.

The offensive tackle has the same technique as the guard on his short set. The tackle normally does not get a tight alignment except on running downs. On first down, he will get a tight 5-technique or maybe a 4-technique alignment. If the defender is tight, he takes the inside or outside step to that alignment and takes him on aggressively. On long-yardage and third-down situations, the defensive ends generally widen their alignments. How wide they go depends on the situation or the personnel playing the position.

If the defender on the tackle is within a yard of his alignment, he has two options. He can take his drop and invite him up the field or he can take the dance step like the guard and take him on. I learned that when I coached at St. Louis.

We had a tackle by the name of Dan Dierdorf. He was a converted guard playing tackle. He had short arms and had very little chance to block a defensive end like "Too Tall" Jones, who played for the Cowboys. He did not drop and take on Too Tall because he could not keep him away from him. He dance stepped out and took him on aggressively. He used the outside-inside-outside steps to get into him. That is where I learned the technique, and I think it is a great change-up for a tackle. Another factor you have to consider is the rhythm of the throw. If the ball is coming out fast, that is a good technique to use.

If the defensive end is extremely wide, the offensive tackle knows where the defender is going. To keep the width of the pocket, the tackle sets with a six-inch, 45-degree-angle step to his outside. He brings the inside foot back and keeps his shoulders square to the line of scrimmage. It is the pocket I talked about earlier. The offensive tackle takes the 45-degree-angle step and works back on a straight line to the point of no return. That generally is the third step of the defensive end. On the third step, the defender has to do something.

By keeping his shoulder square to the line of scrimmage, the offensive tackle can pick up the inside move by the defensive end and drive him inside. That allows the tackle to pick up the tight end stunt between the defensive tackle and end. The best thing the offensive lineman can do is have his shoulder parallel to the line of scrimmage the whole ball game. If the league allowed it, the best pass protection would be field-goal protection. You could get the linemen to go shoe to shoe and stay tight to the line of scrimmage.

The big question last night was: When does the offensive tackle turn in his pass protection drop? If the passing scheme is a five-step scheme, there is a point where the defensive end cannot get under the offensive blocker. If the blocker reaches the point of no return on the pass rush, he can turn and use the inside club with his inside hand to run the defender past the quarterback. If the rusher never tries to bend in across the line that the offensive tackle has established, you do not have to block him.

In 1992 when I was at Green Bay, we had to find a way to get our backs out on the perimeter of the defense. We did not have the same kinds of backs that Bill Walsh had at San Francisco. We needed to get our backs in space, so we studied the screen game. The good screen team that year was Minnesota. We got all the screen tapes we could find and broke them all down. I did the report on the screen game and turned it in to Mike Holmgren. This is the report I made to him.

SCREENS

To be a sound screen team, it is important not to dilute this phase of the game by having too many screens. To keep the defense off-balance, we can utilize various formations, groupings, and movement, but to be effective and to be able to handle multiple fronts and stunts, we need to be consistent with our blocking assignments and the release of the receiving back.

You cannot have too many different types of screens. The screen components must be the same. As a suggestion, with protection being the priority, a sound system of screen blocking would be to block the tight end and release the screening back to the weakside.

Core Elements of Screen Protection

The pass pro pickup assignments should be the same assignments the core group has in its 74/75 protection. The base protection, as it is adjusted to the different fronts, should be executed as far as line shades to alignment and stunts and blitzes are concerned.

The 74/75 protection is a one-back protection scheme we use in our one-back sets (Diagram #3). When we run the screen, we want the tight end to stay in to block and run the screen to the weakside of the formation. When the defense plays their 3 techniques wide and you are trying to get the guards out on the screen, the tackles can slide down and help with the protection. The defender that puts pressure on the screen play is usually the defender covering the backside guard.

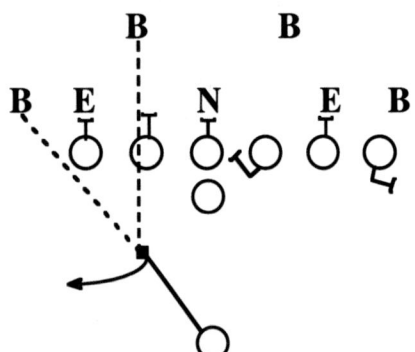

Diagram #3. 74/75 Protection

The core elements of the screen play are the frontside guard, tackle, center, backside guard, quarterback, and running back. The backside tackle

and tight end will be full-time pass blockers. The pass pro pickup for the back is the same as a regular pass play.

If the guard has a 3-technique defender aligned on him, he has to do the same thing he does on regular protection. He cannot do something that gives the play away. The defender has to believe it is a pass play for a screen to work. All our screens came off a five-step rhythm pass. If you are running a screen from a wildcat formation, the timing of the screen will be different.

TIMING

In all the screens we studied, the timing of the linemen was always in question. The linemen would get hung up and not get into the proper position. The back got out too fast or too slow. The key thing in releasing the linemen and the screening back is timing this phase to keep the first force block and the screening back relationship proper. To achieve this, the screening back should set up inside the onside offensive tackle.

He must eyeball his pickup assignment and block him if he rushes using his 74/75 protection technique. At the same time, he must be able to see the onside offensive guard. If the back must block, he must bounce the blitzing linebacker before releasing. He must avoid entanglements that disrupt the timing of his release. If he does not have to block, he must release at the same time the offensive guard releases (this is by sight or by count). If the offensive guard gets entangled, the center will block the first force.

To help with the timing, the back should catch the ball on the move. He should see the playing field numbers to the screenside of the field as a reference point and not run laterally past that point. He should strive to run vertical at the numbers if the force does not show up before that point. Otherwise, he should run inside the first force block of the onside offensive guard or center.

If we teach this concept and coordinate the force blocker's reference point with the numbers, the common fault of the back not setting the force blocker's block up will not be a problem. Of course, when we read man coverage, both the back and the forced blocker must react quicker.

If the offense runs a screen, the first defender to recognize the screen is going to attack it. If the middle linebacker sees the screen, his job is to attack and disrupt the screen. That gives everyone else on the defense time to react and stop the play. The disrupter in the screen could be the linebacker, the free safety, the defensive end who drops off in a fire zone, or the corner. You do not know who will be the disrupter on any screen play. Even if the coverage says the safety will be the one in that area, it could be the linebacker.

The back has to set up inside the offensive tackle. He cannot get outside the tackle. He is not there to chip block on a defender. The best place for the back to be is inside. That lets the tackle know he has help to the inside and can take the pass rusher up the field. If the back comes outside the tackle and chips on the pass rusher, the rusher may go inside the tackle.

The back has to avoid the entanglements that may occur on the play. Linemen will fall on the ground or defenders may try to hold him. It is his job to avoid all those types of problems.

If the back does not have a blitz pickup, he has to release at the same time the force blocker releases. You can do that by sight or by count. To help the timing of the play, we want the back to catch the ball on the run. In our study, we found when the back moved out, stood, caught the ball, and called, "Go" to start the blocking, the timing was poor. The back was too quick or the line was too slow. We want the back to catch the ball on the move and make no verbal call to the linemen.

The back has to be aware of two things. He has to be aware of where the pulling guard or center is and the location of the numbers on the field. He wants to be aware of the numbers because we never want him to run outside the numbers. If he gets to the outside and nothing has happened, he runs north and south up the numbers.

I used to tell Edgar Bennett when he was in Green Bay about the winters. When the snowplows were plowing the streets, if you stepped off the sidewalk, the snowplows ran over you. I told him when he ran the screen, he had to stay on the sidewalk and go north and south. He came off the field one game, and I told him to stay on the sidewalk. Holmgren overheard the reference to the sidewalk and did not know what it was. That was the lingo we had with the offensive line and backs.

He asked me one time during the game to give him a running play. I told him to run 93 blast. He ran the play and it got one yard. He was furious. He was moaning that he did not have any second-and-nine plays. I told him to take one of those second-and-ten plays when you overthrow the son of a gun and run that because it is only a one-yard difference.

The numbers are also the landmark for the blocker who is blocking the force on the play. You and I know that this is clinic talk, and the play does not always happen that way. The guard blocking the force is on a track. He is like a train running down a track. If anyone crosses that track, he blocks him. The back is tied to the pulling guard. If the guard blocks, the back turns up inside his block. If no one crosses the face of the pulling guard, as he reaches the numbers, he turns north and south. The wide receiver to the screenside takes an outside release on the corner to take him out of the play. If the corner rolls, he is the force player on the play and the guard will block him. I handed the report to Mike and we became a screen team in Green Bay. We did a good job of running the screen.

I got a kick out of Mike Maser telling about the way they picked the bad defensive linemen to play in the offensive line at Boston College. At Stanford, you had to lie to the recruits. If Southern Cal was recruiting a player as an offensive tackle, we told him to come to Stanford and we would put him on defense. Brian Holloway was recruited as a defensive lineman. When he got to Stanford, we moved him to the offense.

The next thing I want to get to is the coaching points on the screen.

COACHING POINTS FOR THE SCREEN

All screens will be run with a two-count delay for the offensive and the screen back. The count is one thousand one, one thousand go. In the technical sense of covered linemen, it is hit, extend, and go. The line blocks all pass-rush stunts with normal pass-protection rules.

On-Tackle: Take set based on the defensive end's alignment. Stay with the defensive end except on E-T stunt. Try to lure him upfield, but keep him out of the throwing lane. Keep his hands down.

On-Guard: Take set based on whether you are covered or uncovered. *Covered:* Set block the man over you; release behind the line of scrimmage. Lose your man away from the screenside. You are responsible for first force. *Uncovered:* Set short toward the outside tackle. Release on the count and block the first-force defender. Eyeball the linebacker over you for coverage key.

Center: Take set based on whether you are covered or uncovered. *Covered:* Take the callside away from the man over you. Release, lose your man away from the screenside. If your off-guard is uncovered, he will set behind you looking for the slanting nose tackle. You are the second man out, lead upfield, and block the first man to show. *Uncovered:* Set short toward the on-guard and release on the count; lead upfield and block the first man to show.

Off-Guard: Take set on whether you are covered or uncovered. *Covered:* Set and block the man over you. Release, lose your man away from the screenside. Check for any trailing defenders. If no one shows, turn upfield, look back, and seal inside. *Uncovered:* Set behind the center in a position to help with the slanting nose tackle. Release on the count and block trailers, or turn upfield and seal.

Off-Tackle: Take set on the defensive end's alignment. Stay with him until the screen is thrown. Alert the wide 3-technique position.

Screening Back: The screening back tries to set up inside the onside tackle and release underneath the tackle and his rusher, following the onside guard if possible. The screening back must check his blitz assignment, and if he gets a blitz, he must bounce the blitzing defender before releasing for the pass. In all releases, the back must avoid entanglements that will disrupt the timing of his release. Once the screening back has released, he should be at a depth of four yards and he should catch the ball while on the move.

Tight End: Must be responsible for the offside linebacker as per play or game plan.

Everyone counts differently on the release of the linemen in the screen. We use the count if we are uncovered. If we are covered, we have a block sequence. That is one reason we created the neutral zone with our alignment. When we release on the screen, we hit, extend our arms, and get our butts out on the screen. If we are uncovered, we count one thousand one, one thousand go. The release is a feel thing, and the more you run it, the better you are.

When Don Coryell was with the San Diego Chargers, he had an automatic screen built into his five-step drop. The first thing he wanted to do was throw the ball downfield. If he did not get what he wanted downfield, he threw the quick screen. It was like a hot-pass principle except the guard and center were in front of the back. That was the quick screen, and that was what we wanted to do. We wanted to throw all our screens on that quick rhythm.

The tackle and guard block all the stunts as if they were pass blocking for a throw downfield. We block pass-rush stunts the way we block them. We are not a man scheme or a zone scheme when it comes to line stunts. We block what happens in the stunt. If I am Walter Jones and have to block Jason Taylor, I want to try and take him out of the game. I am not worried about being on the same level as the guard. If I can take him out of the game by being physical, that is what I do.

If the defensive end goes inside, the tackle does not pass him to the guard. He stays on the end unless he is bumped off. It is like basketball. There is a zone concept and a man concept. If you get picked, you switch. If you can fight through the pick, that is the way we play it. We want to be aggressive.

The defense does not always run the E-T stunt with the same rhythm. If the defense has a good tackle, they will delay him on the stunt. They will try to widen the 3 technique and grab the guard to keep him from switching. The defensive tackle on the guard will delay and come off the ball so he can come around to the outside. There are all kinds of rhythms with line stunts.

The on-tackle sets off the alignment of the defensive end. If the defensive end is tight in his alignment, the tackle can short set. If the tackle sees the T-E stunt, he wants to cut the defender off to the inside. He stays on the defensive end throughout the screen except on a T-E stunt. He wants to lure the defensive end up the field and stay on him.

When we first put this play in, we told the tackle to take the defensive end seven yards up the field and cut him. That does not work because of the entanglement of the back in the throwing lane. The defender most likely to make the play on the screen is the defensive end getting off the ground. Since the screen is a delayed play, the defensive end can be a factor if he is not blocked.

The on-guard has a covered and uncovered rule. If he is covered, he short sets and blocks the man over him. When he releases the block to get out, he wants to lose his man away from the screen. It does not happen that way all the time. If he is uncovered, he sets toward the screenside. If he has a linebacker, he sets toward the linebacker. He is responsible for the first force.

If he is uncovered and sets on the linebacker, the linebacker could be the first force. If the guard reads the linebacker squatting in man coverage, that is his first force rule and he goes to block him immediately. You can tell the difference between zone and man coverage by the reaction of the linebacker. If it is zone coverage, the linebacker tilts his hips and drops to his zone. If it is in man coverage, he squats and locks on the running back. If the

linebacker drops out of the cover but the safety shows up, he may become the force.

The guard runs the track to the outside and blocks the force defender. In the NFL, the rules give the linemen a yard over the line of scrimmage before they call the linemen downfield on a pass. In college and high school, you do not have to worry about that.

If the defensive end drops in a fire-zone scheme, he is the first force. The on-tackle reads the defensive end dropping and knows the 3 technique has containment. He sets and waits for him to come to the outside and runs him up the field. He does not have to look for the defender because he will come to him.

In some situations, the wide 3-technique defender may not let the guard release on the screen. The guard will fight like hell to get out, but sometimes he cannot. In that case, the center blocks the first force. You may want to create a call for that situation. We did not because we could read those alignments. When the center has to block the first force, he has to see the linebacker as the guard did.

This is an afterthought: You do not throw the screen in a long-yardage situation. You throw the screen on first or second down. On third down, everyone is looking for the screen and draw.

Let me talk about the center's responsibility. If the center has a nose shaded toward the off-guard, the off-guard has to help the center (Diagram #4). The center cannot snap the ball with his right hand and get a hand on the nose. The off-guard steps down and jams the nose with his inside hand. If the nose is playing to the A gap to his side, he falls back in his set behind the center and takes the nose to the outside and releases the center to go to the screen. If the nose is a two-gap player, we have to do something different. In that case, the nose will try to stay on the center. We give a stay call, and the center stays on the nose while the off-guard switches responsibility with the center. The off-guard becomes the lead blocker or the first force blocker.

Diagram #4. Center/Off-Guard vs. Nose

The off-guard will not get out on the screen too many times. The pressure for the screen comes from the nose tackle or the 3 technique aligned on him. If the nose tackle is a grabber, the off-guard is the next blocker out for the first force block. If the center is uncovered and the defense plays with wide 3 techniques, the center will be out first.

The off-guard is the third blocker out in the screen. If he gets out, he comes down or slightly over the line of scrimmage until he gets to the point where the offensive tackle aligned originally. When he reaches that point, he looks back. If the defensive end has fallen back inside or has gotten off the ground, he blocks him. If there is no one trailing the screen, he turns up the field and seals to the inside. The on-guard has the kick-out, the off-guard has the seal, and the center leads the play. The center leads the back down the numbers.

The receivers going downfield do not look to block. They run their patterns and block at the second level. We do not want them to look to block because it gives the play away, and the secondary can react to the screen. Every screen we call, we call the routes for the receivers first and then we call screen right or left.

If you have a tight end in the pass-protection scheme, it allows the off-guard to get out into the screen more often. The tackle can come down on the 3 technique over the guard, and the tight end can work on the defensive end.

The quarterback takes his quick five-step drop. He stops at five steps and drifts back and delivers the pass to the screen back. If we were to drop seven steps, it gives the defender more time to recognize the screen.

This next part of the screen is the components and faults with the play.

CONSISTENT COMPONENTS

On-Tackle: Get the defensive end upfield seven yards. Get his hands down. If he runs the E-T, pin him inside. *Common Fault:* Cutting causes entanglement with screening back.

On-Guard: Use a good pass set (covered/uncovered). Hit, extend, go. Timing is something you develop with reps. Block first force, key near the linebacker for coverage. Use numbers as a reference point. If the first force is the near the linebacker, block him immediately (man cover). If the first force has not tried to attack the screening back before you reach the numbers, sprint to the numbers and start to move vertically. Look for the first defender. *Common Faults:* Blocks too long at the line of scrimmage; slow getting out on screen. Sprint is too flat and not using numbers as a reference point

Center: Good set. Second man out on the screen unless on-guard gets hung up. Use numbers as a reference point. Use the same coaching points as the playside guard. Use the stay call. *Common Faults:* Blocks too long at the line of scrimmage; slow getting out on screen.

Off-Guard: Good set. Third man out on screen. The timing of this block must be held slightly longer than those of the center and playside guard. You need to slow the rusher down to allow the quarterback to get set. As the third man out, you are responsible for any trailing defender. Sprint to the onside tackle's original alignment and block the MDM (most dangerous man) or seal off the inside for the screening back's running lane. *Common Fault:* Failing to check for trailers.

Off-Tackle: Take on the defensive end and protect the quarterback. *Common Fault:* Not blocking the play as a regular pass play.

Tight End: Generally assigned to the offside linebacker on the screen called or by the game plan. Must take the proper angle to the cutoff point to position yourself between the defender and the screening back. *Common Faults:* Poor angle to the linebacker or losing sight of defender.

This next diagram will show you how we use the numbers as reference points (Diagram #5). In the collegiate or professional game, the number references will not change. However, for Canadian football, the numbers will change because their field is wider than ours. In Canada, they use the goalposts as reference points. They are about the same width as the hash marks in professional football. This formation is a split back set. The play is *24 halfback, screen left.*

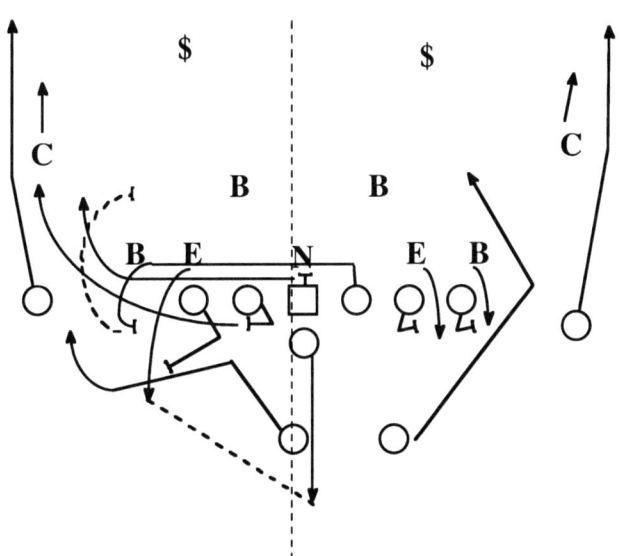

Diagram #5. Screen Left

The onside tackle takes the defensive end wherever he wants to go. The screen back sets up inside the tackle and latches onto the onside guard. The onside guard keys the Will linebacker. He reads his drop to see if he could be the force. If he locks on the screen back, the guard goes to block him immediately. If he does not come, he sprints down the line to the numbers on his track.

The screen back comes out and catches the ball over his shoulder. He sees the force block and follows it for his cut. If there is no force defender, he continues to the numbers and cuts upfield. The center comes out and leads the screen back up the field. He may be slightly over the line of scrimmage as he releases downfield. The off-guard is the third blocker out and seals the inside.

If this were Don Coryell, he would take the five-step drop with his quarterback (Diagram #6). The tight end would run a pattern over the ball, and the split end would run an out pattern. They would be the primary receivers. If the Will linebacker blitzed, he hit the tight end in that area. If the linebacker did not come, he dropped the ball off to the back on the screen.

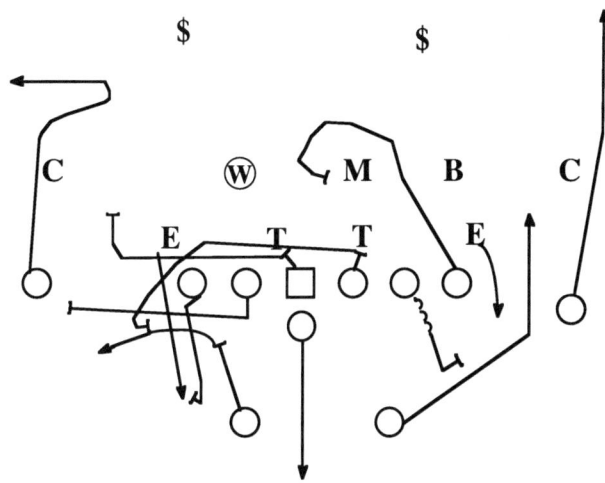

Diagram #6. Coryell Screen

Those are the details of the screen, but how do you practice it? Like anything else, you have to walk before you run. The problem with professional football is contending with what little time you have to work on what you need to. In training camp, we might run this particular screen four times. You have to get the play into the offense and run it in the ball games. Stuff is going to happen in a football game. It is like they always say, "It happens." In a game, you set the screen up and expect the force to come from a particular defender and it comes from someone else. However, if you follow the rules for the play, it should work out fine.

In practice, we work half line and run two drills at the same time working the screen to both sides (Diagram #7). In the drill, you need the on-tackle, guard, center, and off-guard. The key is the defensive personnel you use in the drill. You have to give the offensive linemen all the different looks they will see in a game. To start with I will align the defense in a 4-3 alignment.

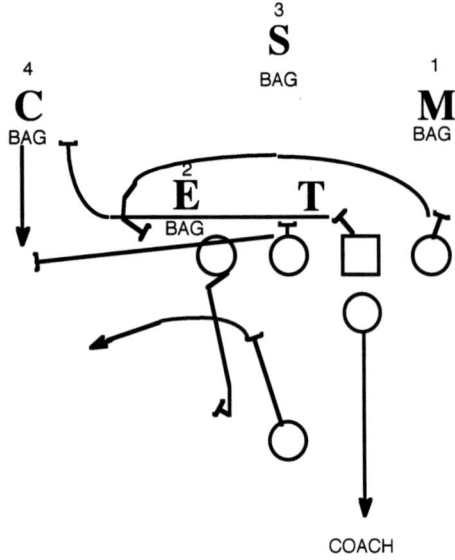

Diagram #7. Screen Drill

You give the Mike linebacker, defensive end, safety, and corner a hand dummy. That way the offense does not know who the force defender will be. The coach stands behind the offensive line and designates the force player he wants. We snap the ball, and the force player covers his responsibility. The linemen go through their blocking scheme on the screen. After we do the rep, we run the play again and change the force defender.

The offensive linemen are doing the same thing each time and applying their rules to pick up the force defender (Diagram #8). When you drop the defensive end into the fire-blitz scheme, make sure you bring the defensive tackle to the outside for containment. That gives the offensive tackle the work he needs.

Make sure you go through each situation with all the possible force defenders coming to force. When you teach it, you have to *walk it, talk it,* and *run it.* The drill will never be as fast as you want it because every time you give someone a bag, they take their foot off the accelerator. However, that is the way to teach it.

The screen is a running drive block for the first man out. That is the reason for the bags. You want the linemen to block the bags and not pussyfoot about what they are doing. To get effective with anything you do, you must rep it repeatedly.

In a professional football game, we get 63 to 65 plays. We will throw the ball at least 40 times. That leaves 20 plays. If you have three plays for short yardage and two plays for goal line, that leaves 15 plays where the linemen get to run the football. When you run these plays, you want to be efficient. You want to do something that you know how to do. Our number one run was *93 blast.* That was our weakside lead play. We came off the ball and zone blocked the play. It was a simple play but when we needed three yards, that is the play we called. I am getting off the subject.

If you practice the screen and rep it, your players will gain confidence in it. When you gain confidence in the play, you will get better at it. Talking about plays, I want to show you one that is the staple of the West Coast offense. This is called *18 Bob* (Diagram #9). This was a super play against the vanilla 4-3 or 3-4 defense. I will show it to you from the 3-4 front.

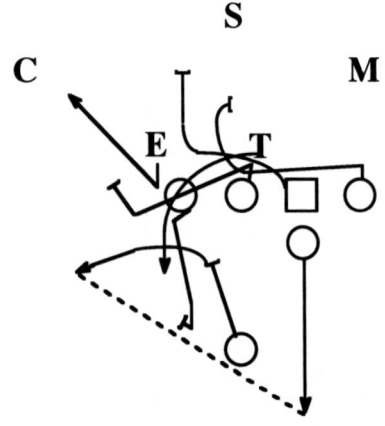

Diagram #8. Fire-Zone Blitz

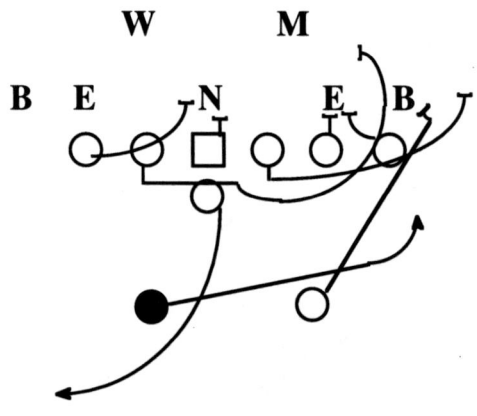

Diagram #9. 18 Bob

The onside tackle steps into the neutral zone inside the defensive end with his eyes on the Mike linebacker. If the Mike linebacker fires the gap, the tackle blocks him. The tight end steps into the neutral zone at the defensive end aligned in the 5 technique. If the linebacker does not blow the B gap, we double-team the 5-tecchnique defender with the tackle and tight end.

When we double-team, we want to get vertical push off the line of scrimmage back into the linebacker. We want the linebacker to have to jump over the top of the double-team to get to the outside. We do not want him to come downhill and snot bubble the pulling guard. The tackle steps inside with his first step to eyeball the linebacker. On the second step, he wants to be hip to hip with the tight end coming down on the double-team. When he steps inside, he has to get his second step down or he will lose his base and get whipped by the defensive end. One of them eventually will come off for the backside linebacker. The fullback attacks the outside linebacker and uses what we call a *Bob block*. He wants to take out the outside knee of the outside linebacker.

The frontside guard pulls and gets on the perimeter. He has to take his weight off the outside foot so he can move it. He pivots off his inside foot and turns the foot to the outside. He does not want to come flat with the inside foot because that is not the way the knee is made. When he pivots with the inside foot, he will make a divot. If you are a golfer, you will know what that means. He makes his lead step with his outside foot. He picks it up and puts it down in the direction he is going. On the next step, he moves to the outside.

He has one problem on the pull. He has to let the fullback clear. He has to take a small bubble step as he goes to the perimeter. The center base blocks on the nose tackle. The backside guard pulls using a shallow technique to avoid the quarterback. After he passes the quarterback, he bubbles a little in his track to the outside. If there is a pile in the hole, he blows it up. His block is the frontside inside linebacker.

The backside tackle comes down and scoops the area from his position to the nose tackle. He wants to seal for the pulling guard. Normally, he blocks the backside defensive end trying to get inside. If the defense slants the nose tackle to the backside, the offensive tackle could end up clipping the nose tackle.

When the defenses started getting sophisticated, they stopped that play. That became one of our problems and why we went to the screen game to get to the perimeter.

I am going to show you some of the plays on tape. I will call the play for you, run it, and talk about it. We call this play *red right, 22 Texas, halfback screen left* (Diagram #10). Red right is the formation. The pass is 22 Texas, and the play is halfback screen left. The formation is a pro set right with a split back alignment in the backfield. The defense aligns in a standard 4-3 under front.

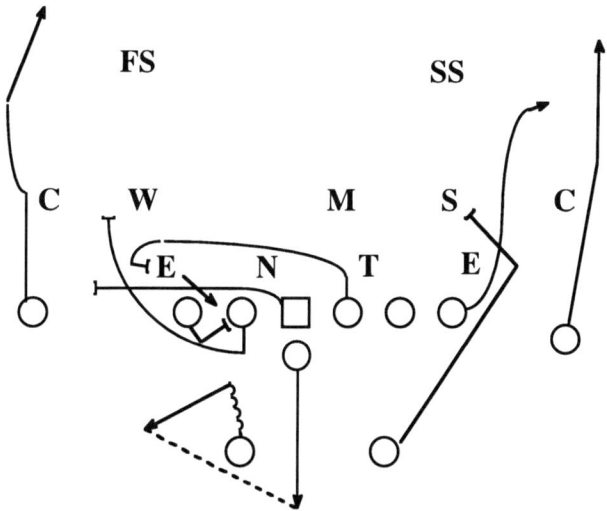

Diagram #10. 22 Texas, Screen Left

The fullback to the tight end side runs a scat route as designed in the 22 Texas pass. On the play, the 5-technique defensive end to the openside slants to the inside and prevents the guard from getting out on the screen to block the force. The center gets out and becomes the force defender blocker.

The on-guard gets off the slanting tackle and takes the center's responsible as the lead blocker.

The off-guard comes down the line of scrimmage and cleans up the defender chasing the play.

On the second play, it is the same formation except it is red left, screen right. The on-guard is uncovered, but the center has a shade aligned to that side. The guard sets to the linebacker; however, he gets a hand on the shade defender so the protection is sound. As the on-guard pulls for the force defender, he commits one of the common faults of the force defender blocker. He gets outside the numbers and allows the corner to get across his face and make the tackle.

The third play is the same play, but we are in the red zone. People used to say you cannot run screens in the red zone. They thought the play was too slow to develop. If you throw the five-step rhythm screen, it is a good play. We were good in the red zone with the screen play. One year on Monday Night Football against Philadelphia, we scored three touchdowns in the red zone on screen plays. You can run the screens in the red zone, but it is all timing. If you watch the receivers, they are running their routes. They are not thinking about blocking.

The next play is a fullback screen right (Diagram #11). The formation is a blue formation right with jet motion. The wide receivers are on the line of scrimmage, and the tight end is set in the tight slot to the shortside of the formation. The fullback is behind the quarterback, and the halfback is to the screenside.

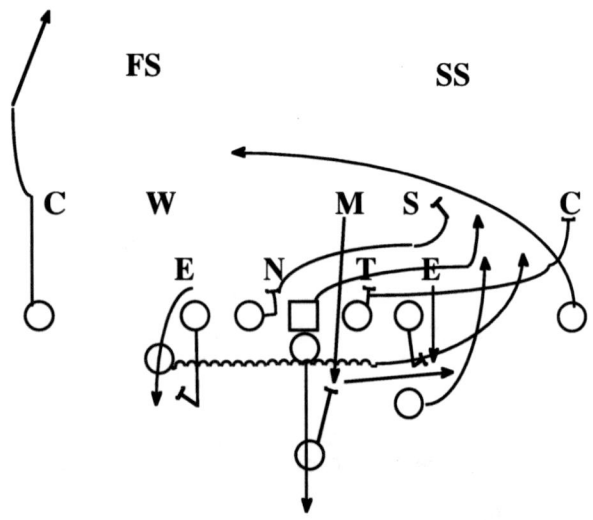

Diagram #11. Fullback Screen Right

The components of a screen never change. The on-guard does the same thing whether he aligns left or right. If he is the on-guard to the direction of the screen, he has the force defender. The center is the lead blocker, and the off-guard is the cleanup blocker. On this play, the defense plays a man-free coverage and blitzes the linebacker to the side of the screen. The fullback has the linebacker blitz as part of his protection package. He steps up and bounces the blitzing linebacker before he releases into the screen.

The on-guard gets out on the force and is in good shape but makes a mistake. When you block the force, you do not jump the defender playing the force. The guard gets to the numbers and turns upfield. Make the force defender come to the guard to make the tackle. Make him run through the guard to get to the ballcarrier. The guard chases the defender outside the numbers and misses the block. The center coming behind him has to clean up his block or the play will get more yardage.

Andy Reid was our tight ends coach at Green Bay when I was there. He was in the booth and I was on the field. We were in communication with each other. Coach Holmgren had a four-way headset and could listen to all of us. We played the 49ers in the playoffs in Green Bay and were ahead 14-0 at halftime. We felt good about what was happening.

Desmond Howard was our return man. He got hurt in the first half, and we did not have a return man to start the second half. We put in Andre Rison to return the second-half kickoff. He fumbled at the 15-yard line. They scored and made the score 14-7. We took the ball and ran it up their nose and got into the red zone. Mike threw two incomplete passes, and we had to settle for a field goal. The offensive line came off the field and was upset because we did not punch the ball in with the run.

I was talking to Andy in the box. I told him that is just like life in the NFL. We drive the ball down the field and that dumbass throws two passes in the red zone. Coach Holmgren *yelled* into the headset, "Who said that?" Andy told me, "Tom, you are on the wrong line." There was no more of that going on.

The next play is a *zebra set*, which is a one-back set (Diagram #12). The formation is a trips tight end set right. We run two-jet motion, which is the wide receiver to the trips side coming in motion back to the set. The play is a fullback screen right. The secondary is in two-deep zone coverage. We have two blockers out on the field running in convoy, but the screen back ran right by them. He was a running back, and the linemen could not keep up with him. He almost broke the play by using his speed. The back has to use his judgment with the blocker. If he can see open field, he takes it.

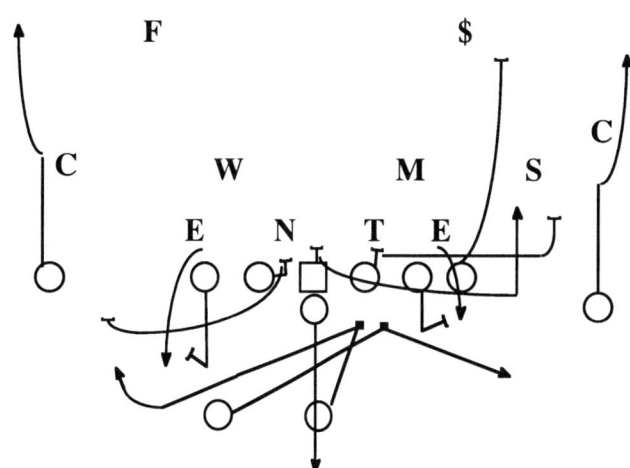

Diagram #13. Double Screen

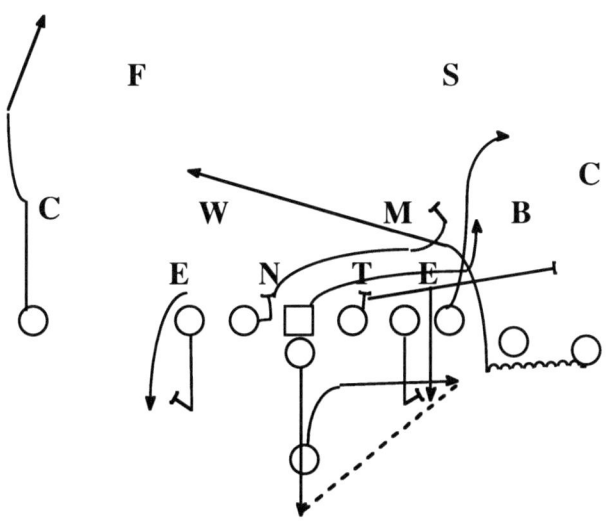

Diagram #12. Zebra Screen

The next play is run off a lead draw fake. We call it *brown right, fake fox two run, double screen right"* (Diagram #13). The fox two is the name of the lead draw. The fullback fakes the lead draw up inside and filters out to the left side of the formation. The tailback fakes the draw and releases to the right. The center and right guard form the screening blocking to the right and the left guard leads the screen to the left. The quarterback has a choice of sides to throw the ball. We have a one-man screen to the left and a two-man screen to the right.

All the offensive linemen are concerned with is the screen direction. The rest of the call is window dressing. We call the entire play so the receivers run the routes that we call. The play must look like a pass play for the screen to be successful. When we get into the red zone, we want to throw the screen off our best red zone pass. The defense will work their butts off to stop that play. That makes the screen a good call in the red zone. The defense gets extra defenders into the scheme to stop your favorite pass. That leaves fewer defenders to pick up the screen.

Thank you gentlemen, I enjoyed my time. I hope you got something out of it.

ABOUT THE AUTHOR

Tom Lovat's coaching experience includes 41 years of service, two Super Bowl trips, and a Super Bowl championship. Lovat retired after five seasons as the run game coordinator and offensive line coach of the Seattle Seahawks.

Lovat spent 12 seasons as the offensive line coach under head foot-ball coach, Mike Holmgren. From 1992 to 1998, Lovat was the offensive line coach for the Green Bay Packers. After the 1998 season, he followed head coach Mike Holmgren from the Packers to coach the Seattle Seahawks' offensive line. Five years later, Lovat retired.

A veteran of more than 20 NFL Scouting Combines, he serves as a consultant for the IMG agency, preparing an offensive lineman's technique, mental abilities, and physical skills for combine-specific drills.

In 2005, the Seahawks drafted his pupil, center Chris Spencer, in the first round, and the Dallas Cowboys selected offensive tackle Rob Petitti in the sixth round. In 2006, Tampa Bay drafted another pupil, Boston College offensive tackle Jeremy Trueblood, in the second round.

Lovat started coaching at Utah. There, he became the defensive line coach in 1967. Next, he went to Idaho State University (1968 to 1970), coaching the defensive secondary and offensive line. Lovat moved on to the Canadian Football League as the defensive coordinator for the Ottawa Rough Riders in 1971 before returning to Utah as an assistant for the 1972 to 1973 seasons. He became the head coach at Utah from 1974 to 1976.

Next, Lovat coached at Stanford University from 1977 to 1979 with Bill Walsh. He was then hired by Bart Starr of the Green Bay Packers as the assistant offensive line coach in 1980. He went on to the St. Louis Cardinals under Jim Hanifan from 1981 to 1984 as line coach. Then, he coached the Indianapolis Colts from 1985 to 1988. He came back to the Cardinals when the team moved to Phoenix, coaching under Joe Bugel as his line coach from 1990 to 1991.

The former Packers coach resides in Appleton, Wisconsin, but spends summers at his Eagle River cottage. His son, Mark, currently serves as the Packers' assistant strength and conditioning coach.

LOVAT AT A GLANCE

- 1999-2003: Seattle Seahawks, Offensive Line Coach
- 1992-1998: Green Bay Packers, Offensive Line Coach
- 1990-1991: Phoenix Cardinals, Offensive Line Coach
- 1985-1988: Indianapolis Colts, Offensive Line Coach
- 1981-1984: St. Louis Cardinals, Offensive Line Coach
- 1980: Green Bay Packers, Offensive Line Coach
- 1977-1979: Stanford University, Offensive Line Coach
- 1974-1976: University of Utah, Head Football Coach
- 1972-1973: University of Utah, Offensive Line Coach
- 1971: Ottawa Rough Riders, Defensive Coordinator
- 1968-1970: Idaho State University, Offensive Line Coach
- 1967: University of Utah, Defensive Line Coach

BUILDING THE OFFENSIVE LINE/THE RAP DRAW AND WILDCAT PLAYS

Miami Dolphins

I want to thank Bob for asking me to come and share some ideas with you today. I have been sitting around on my butt since January 19th. I have not talked a lot of football to anyone. This will be the first time I have talked football in a long time.

How many guys in here play golf? When you go out and play golf, you have to fight with your wife all the time. You spend four hours on the course with your buddies. You smoke cigars, drink a little beer, and raise a little hell. The bottom line is this: When you play golf, your wife is mad at you all the time. This is a story about a coach walking down the street. A panhandler stopped him. The panhandler was disgusting. His clothes were shabby, he smelled bad, and he had not shaved in a month. However, the guy felt sorry for him and pulled a 10-dollar bill out of his wallet.

The panhandler got excited at the sight of the 10-dollar bill. The guy told the panhandler if he gave him the 10-dollar bill, he knew he would go immediately to the liquor store and buy a bottle of booze. The panhandler told him he would not do that because he needed a meal and a place to get some sleep. The panhandler told him he quit drinking five years ago.

The guy is still holding the 10 dollars in his hand. He told the panhandler, if he gave him the 10 bucks, he would run over to the convenience store and buy a carton of cigarettes. The panhandler told him he would not do that either because he quit smoking 10 years ago. The guy continued to question the panhandler about how he would spend the 10 dollars. He asked him if he gave him the 10 dollars, would he try to pick up a streetwalker and engage in her trades. The panhandler told him he would not do that because it had been 15 years since he had sex.

He finally said if he gave the panhandler the 10 dollars, he would go to the golf course, gamble it on the game, and lose it. The panhandler told him he had not played golf in 20 years. With that, the guy put the 10 dollars back in his wallet. The panhandler was confused and wanted to know what was going on. The guy told him, he was going to take him home to his house, get him a home-cooked meal, and get him cleaned up. He wanted his wife to see what happens to a guy who gives up drinking, smoking, sex, and golf.

I want to talk to you about offensive line fundamentals. I am a big fundamentals coach. I have always been that type of coach—one that believes in fundamentals. I think that fundamentals are the key to what we are doing as far as football is concerned. One of the things I want to show you is what I call a *mission statement*. It is a statement I have given to the players that I have coached. I have coached for over 35 years, and I have never coached anything but the offensive line. I have never coached quarterbacks, running backs, or wide receivers, and I do not know if I could even deal with those players. I have coached the offensive line for 35 to 40 years, and I believe what we do is the most important thing on a football team. It is the most important thing because without the offensive line, you cannot play the game. I tell my players that all the time.

You can go out and play 7-on-7, and that gets boring after a while. I remember sitting in a room with the other coaches watching tape of a 7-on-7 drill. It was so boring that I went to sleep. However, when you put the big guys into the drill, it becomes a physical-confrontation sport, and that is what football is all about. That is what draws people to the games. There is combat involved between the offensive and defensive lines.

What we are doing as offensive line coaches is creating people who believe in themselves, working like hell, and doing it for absolutely no recognition. I worked for Jack Bicknell for 12 years. Jack always said if he were going to start a business, the first people he would want to get involved would be offensive linemen. He believed that, and I do too. Offensive linemen are the most important people on the field.

In order to play the game, you have to be physically tough and demanding of yourself. You have to understand that there are fundamentals and techniques involved in playing the game that are as unnatural as anything you have ever done. You do not walk down the street, cross the street, and punch somebody in the mouth. It is socially unacceptable. Offensive linemen have to understand that they have to get into the defensive linemen and knock the crap out of them for 60 minutes. They have to try to physically dominate the defenders. That is something that is not socially acceptable.

It is not like the athletic pursuits of the wide receivers, running backs, and quarterbacks. The running, throwing, and catching are athletic skills. What we teach the offensive linemen is unnatural.

Individual technique is very important. I talk about techniques and how they pertain to the other players. If the player can master the techniques, he can become as good as he can possibly be. We are always talking "self-actualization." That refers to a player reaching his full potential—not many players do that. The job of the offensive line coach is to prepare the players to be the best they can be.

MISSION STATEMENT

The offensive line must be fundamentally sound and tough; each individual must know what is expected of him to master those requirements. Blocking can be developed to a greater sense than the other phases of football because it is the most unnatural task. It requires many hours of hard work because there are more aspects to learn.

The more techniques you can master, the easier it will be to cope with various situations. These facts must be accepted as a way of life for a blocker, and success can only be achieved with tremendous confidence in one's ability. Concentration, self-discipline, and a willingness to pay the price are part of being an offensive lineman.

Determined, intelligent, and aggressive blocking are indispensable qualities of a great football team from both a technical and psychological standpoint. It is difficult for a team to have outstanding morale, confidence, and enthusiasm when it lacks the ability to sustain a great ground game or provide adequate protection for the passer.

The offensive line coach is always dealing with what's leftover. We have all been there at one time or another. When I was at Boston College, the defensive line coach got the pick of the litter. The players rolled off the bus, the defensive line coach got the players he wanted, and I got the players that were left. We would be practicing on the sled and working on the boards, and every so often another soldier from the defensive side would join our ranks. He could not make it with the defensive line, so they sent him to the offensive line.

When I was in college, my coach told me the offensive line was the last stop before the bus stop. Before a player was thrown off the team, the offensive line was his last chance of staying on the team if he was a lineman. Those are the things that create the comradeship that exists on the offensive line. As an offensive line coach, I try to foster those things with my players. I think it is important that we all try to do that with our players. I saw a guy last night wearing a T-shirt that said, "Offensive Lineman: The Only Real Skilled Position."

I used to give my players at Boston College special T-shirts at the end of training camp. None of the other position coaches gave their players anything like that. It was a big deal involving the comradeship in the offensive line.

The last paragraph of the mission statement is important because it shows the game cannot be played without the offensive line. The offensive line is not a necessary evil. We are one of the most integral parts of what is happening on the football field. As coaches, we try to stress that point. You coaches are a prime example of that statement. When I come to these clinics and see all you guys trying to learn and sharing ideas about offensive line play, it emphasizes that fact.

BLOCKING

- We must develop tough, aggressive, intelligent blocking. We want our enemies hit. Do not confuse this with finesse blocking or influence techniques where we endeavor to guide a defensive man's actions to help a particular play.
- We will work fundamentally on blocks that we want executed. Never sacrifice the "blow" for the sake of thinking about techniques.
- You must have individual pride. Strive to be the best blocker in football.
- You must have pride: team, unit, self. Strive to contribute and be the best line in professional football.
- You must know the complete play in order to end up in the proper position.
- Blocking is a matter of pride and desire. Refuse to be whipped by the defensive man. An upper hand can be gained by mentally intimidating the defender.
- Effective line play begins in the huddle.

When we talk about the offensive line, we have to talk about blocking. The first thing the offensive line has to be is tough and physical. We have to get after people, and we have to want to knock the defender on his butt. It is not something that you *have* to do; it is something that you *want* to do. We do not want to catch a defender, we want to hit people. We are going to be physical and control the line of scrimmage, and we are going to try to dominate our opponents both physically and mentally. We are going to do that through a constant process of pressure.

We want to work on the fundamentals of blocks because blocking is an unnatural skill. These skills can be performed to a higher level, and more ability can be created because these are unnatural tasks—they are not something that players are naturally, athletically inclined to do. They are unnatural, and if you work at them long enough, you will improve.

You must have individual pride as a player. You must believe in yourself and understand what your job is. The offensive lineman's job is to go on the field every day, do his job the right way, and get better at it all the time.

You must have pride in *team, unit, self.* The team always comes first. The next aspect of pride is within the offensive line as a unit, and self is last in our expression of pride. Pride is a very important part of being an offensive lineman.

I am a firm believer in the big picture. I want my players to know what is going on around them. I am not interested in players that only know what *they* are supposed to do. They have to know what the people around them are doing. They have to know what the other linemen and the running backs are doing. They need to know what the quarterback is doing and where he is looking. They have to know the complete play to end up in the right spot.

Blocking is a matter of pride and desire. It is refusing to be whipped by the defensive player. The upper hand can be gained by mentally intimidating the opponent. The way to do that is to stay on his butt like a bulldog all night. The offensive lineman will not let go of the defender. He stays after him all night long.

You may play 60 plays in a game, and the defender will win some of those plays. He will win some of the battles you engage in. But if the offensive lineman stays after the defender long enough, he will win the war.

Effective line play begins in the huddle with the quarterback calling a play. As the quarterback calls the play, the lineman starts processing it in his mind. He gets a mental picture of the play that has been called. He knows what everyone around him is going to do. The next thing he considers is what the defense is going to do. When he gets to the line of scrimmage, it becomes a stimulus response to the situation.

Upon hearing the play from the quarterback, the offensive lineman visualizes his assignment. He has to think about possible adjustments and calls that may occur at the line of scrimmage. As he is processing all these things in his mind, he has to continually keep the snap count in mind. He cannot forget the snap count.

If the offensive lineman is slow coming off the ball, he will get whipped. It is impossible for an offensive lineman to be aggressive when he is uncertain of his assignment. He must know what he is doing. I stand behind the offensive line in practice, and I can always tell when things are going to be bad. I see two offensive linemen at the line of scrimmage looking around at each other. That means at least one of them is looking for help.

My offensive line coach used to tell us all the time, "You never want to get to the line of scrimmage and play switch 'em." That was an expression he used to relay a thought about indecision. It refers to having two thumbs. You have one thumb in your mouth and one in your butt and you do not want to switch 'em. You want to get to the line of scrimmage and know what is going on.

The difference between a great block and a fair one is the fraction of time between contact and follow-through. There are a number of reasons why a blocker fails.

BLOCKING FAILURES AND CAUSES

- Ignorance of assignment
- Loafing
- Tipping—failure to master the stance
- Lack of aggressiveness
- Not off on the count

There is a correct and incorrect way of executing every block. I will not permit a substitute technique to be used in a block. I have had players who played for me over the years that did things their way. I did not coach them a lot. Tony Boselli was one of those players. I told him what color jersey we were wearing for practice and let him do his own thing. Leon Searcy played for me for four or five years. He was a great football player. He was an aggressive, tough, and nasty football player. I did not coach him. He had a bunch of wild things he did. I told him, "There's the field—make sure you get there on time." When we went in to watch film, we had Boselli on one side and Searcy on the other. I told the younger players, if they wanted to be a technical player, they needed to watch Boselli. I told them not to look at Leon because he had his own way of doing things. However, I try to stay on top of the players to make them "technique sound."

The old rule about the blocker keeping his head between the defender and the ballcarrier still holds as a sound rule. The blocker has to keep his body in position and make the defender escape around behind the blocker. The blocker has to have a good fundamental knowledge of basic defensive alignment.

The defenses today do not simply align in a 4-3 or 3-4. The defensive players spend as much time in the film room as we do. They are constantly scheming and trying to stop the offense. The offensive linemen have to know defensive alignments and recognize what they are doing. I was sitting in the back of the room last night listening to the question-and-answer session. Coaches were talking about different situations and alignments. You have to coach your players that way. They have to be aware of situations that differ from basic alignments.

I remember one question about what you are supposed to do on the backside of a power play when the defense runs a T-E stunt. If there is a wide 3-technique defender to the backside, I coach my center to slow down on his back block toward the 3 technique. The backside tackle has to step in deeper to protect himself against the defensive end if they run the T-E stunt. When studying film, you constantly look for that basic alignment situation. You have to be aware of that situation because of their alignment. The players must have a good knowledge of basic defensive alignment so they can recognize those situations when they occur in a game.

In the NFL, when you play teams twice a year, you should build a book. Write down what the defenders do against you the first time you play them. Write down the defenders' favorite moves and study them. When you play them again, you will find out whether the defender is a creature of habit or a player that changes things up with his play. I want to stress this last point. *Once we establish a strong running game and a consistent rushing attack, and we can defend the line of scrimmage and protect the quarterback, there will be titles, championships, and a feeling of pride and togetherness that can never be taken away.* I believe that wholeheartedly—that is absolutely the truth.

Fifteen years from now, my players will be together drinking beer somewhere and remembering the days when they accomplished all those great things because of the togetherness. The offensive line is one of the areas where that truly takes place. The offensive line is a club—a group in which the members take great pride in what they do and believe in each other. That is an attitude we have to create and constantly build within their minds. As the younger players come up, you must make them understand that the offensive line is an important part and not a necessary evil of a football team. They must understand the offensive line is the most important part of a football team.

I want to get into the football aspect of this lecture. I am a technical and fundamentals coach. I believe stance and start are two of the most common fundamentals abused in situations. One of the things I want to talk about is stance. I think stance is very important. I have been told that you can only build a skyscraper on a proper foundation. If you want to go up, you must have a proper foundation. You can build an outhouse on anything. The stance is the foundation of the offensive lineman.

I believe in a balanced stance. I want the feet shoulder-width apart. What does that mean? Shoulder-width apart for the feet means the toes are underneath the armpits. I am a narrow-stance coach. I believe you must have a narrow stance to do all the things a lineman needs to do. The good linemen I coached over the years had narrow stances. Tony Boselli was the best football player I ever coached, and he had a narrow stance. He was 6'8" and 320 pounds, and his feet were never wider than 18 to 20 inches apart.

I believe you must have your feet up under your body. When you squat, you develop the most power straight up and down off your knees and hips. You do not squat with your feet nine miles apart. You cannot develop any power that way. The body levers are not built that way. To produce power, you must have your feet under your body.

Their feet, in the stance, are pointed straight ahead with the balance on the inside of their feet. I let the players take a toe-to-instep stagger if they need it. I want their feet as close to parallel as possible. When going down in the stance, I want their elbows to rest on their knees for balance. When the player puts his hand on the ground, I tell him to place it as if his eyeball fell out of its socket and he is reaching down to pick it up.

There should be six to eight inches between the ground, hand, elbow, and knee. Their feet should be almost flat on the ground. You should not be able to slip a piece of paper under the heels of the linemen. I do not want any high toe raises with their feet. A high toe raise tells me the lineman is not very flexible in his hips. Their knees should be under their shoulders and straight ahead. I do not want their knees turned out. By placing their weight on the inside of their feet, it forces the linemen to get their knees under their shoulders.

There is very little weight placed on the hand, and most of the weight is equally distributed between the feet. That allows the lineman to move in any direction he has to. From this position, he can balance step, pull, go straight ahead, or whatever he has to do.

Defensive players are taught to read the stances of the offensive linemen just like offensive linemen read the stances of defenders. That requires a lineman to take the same stance every time he gets down. He cannot take a different stance to perform different tasks. He wants to avoid tipping anything and giving away what he is going to do. We want the lineman to do the same thing repeatedly in his stance. We want to develop consistency. He has to play and practice in the same stance. He has to be the same guy from day to day both mentally and physically.

The offensive linemen have to work on getting better. If they stay the same, they are getting worse. They have to maintain a situation where they are working on getting better. Every year that I have coached, I have started every practice with a stance and start drill. It is like clockwork every day.

When you practice the start, you take a different start on every rep. You do not want them simply going straight ahead. We use lateral lead steps, drop-steps for positions, set-and-go steps, or whatever you want to work on that day. Change up the steps from day to day. I want the linemen to think. I do not want them to be robots. You want to cover as many possible situations as you can. That allows us to work on specific techniques and footwork.

When I talk about a straight-ahead start, I want to get the feet at shoulder-width apart and the elbows on the knees for balance. When the grounded hand goes to the ground, the off elbow stays on the knee. The feet are flat on the ground. I am 62 years old, and I can do this. In high school and college, the players are young and flexible. Get them to do this. If they are physically incapable of keeping their feet on the ground by keeping their knees inside their bodies, you have problems. You are talking about a lineman who is not physically able to do a particular task.

The other thing I see all the time is teams that play without getting in a three-point stance. The spread offenses have put the offensive linemen in a two-point stance. I have to go along with that. I am not going to fight that type of technique. The problem is when a player moves from one level to another. If a player moves from high school to the college level or from college to the pro level, he may have a problem. If he has played in a system where he has never had his hand in the dirt, he could have some problems. If the new coach says, "Get in a three-point stance," it is like starting from scratch.

I would encourage you to try and get the coach who is in charge of the offense to do some things from the three-point stance. If a player is moving on to the next level, you are doing him a disservice if you do not teach him that. He could be going to a conventional offense and not have the skills and techniques to be successful.

Getting into a proper stance is the most important thing. We want them in proper alignment and takeoff. When they are taking off straight ahead, the first step is six inches. Everyone does the six-inch takeoff drill. I use boards. I have my players take off and step over the width of the board, which is six inches. If your takeoff step is long, you increase the time it takes to get the second step on the ground.

The offensive lineman that can get the second step on the ground quickly has an advantage in the block. When he takes the first step, his toes and knee should be in a straight line. When we do drill work, I stand to the side and watch those first steps. I want to make sure no one has their toes way out in front of their knees.

In the stance, the offensive lineman has to bow his neck and look through his eyebrows. He should be able to see the feet of a defender three yards away from him. If he lifts his head to see where the defender aligns, his tail goes down and he is not in the proper position.

The player has to able to "think" the weight from one foot to the other. If a player moves his right foot first, he has to think the weight is off that foot and mentally shift it to the left side. He must be able to step with either foot equally well. That is the reason we align in a parallel stance.

We have vertical and horizontal splits. A vertical split is the distance you are off the ball. As a rule, the guard's split is toes to the heels of the center. The tackle aligns with his toes on the toes of the guard. If we are on the goal line or short yardage, we may push the split up on the ball. We align with a maximum vertical split. In that split, the helmet of the guard is on the belt line of the center.

If the offensive lineman needs to pull, he can pull either way because he is in a parallel stance. If he has a big stagger in his feet, he cannot pull the same to the right and left. There are a lot of coaches that teach the skip-pull (Diagram #1). I used the skip-pull if the lineman had to fold around an adjacent player. In the skip-pull, the shoulders stay parallel to the line of scrimmage and the lineman folds to the outside.

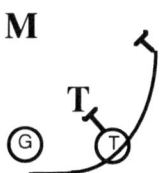

Diagram #1. Skip-Pull

If the lineman is doing a long pull, he has to open his hips to the target. On the power play, we use the long pull (Diagram #2). The guard opens his hips to the target and gets his eyes in the position he is going. The job of the guard on the power play is to swab out the hole. That means the guard is reading the block of the fullback on the outside linebacker. If the outside linebacker closes the fullback down and has his inside arm hanging free, we tell the guard to blow him up. If the defender squeezes down, the linebacker is going out over the top.

Diagram #2. Long Pull

We told the guard to swab out the hole. The only way he ever went outside of everyone was if there was no place to fit him on the inside. If he could not see the inside arm of the outside linebacker and there was no place to fit, he bounced to the outside. I heard the coach last night talking about the back bouncing outside on the power play. We tell the back if he goes to the outside, he is on his own. It is buyer beware for him. We do not want to take the back to the outside if we do not have to.

When I taught the long pull, I lined the linemen up with their feet against a yard line to the side they were pulling. If a lineman pulled to his right, he threw his right elbow back as if he were rebounding a basketball. He threw his elbow, opened his hips, and stepped with his right foot over the line. He pivoted on his left foot and drove threw with his back foot and hand. We used to do that drill every day going in both directions. In doing these drills, we were constantly striving for perfection.

After we taught stance and start, we went to a *block progression*. The block progression was teaching the basic concepts of the block (Diagram #3). We always taught the progression from the block going backward. I need two volunteers to show you this drill. The blocker gets in a football position with his tail down and his head up. The defender walks into the blocker. The blocker gets his hands into the chest of the defender and his head centered on his breastplate. The defender reaches down and grasps the blocker under his elbows. That is the perfect fitted position, and that is what we want the blocker to feel.

Diagram #3. Fitted Position

I play a lot of golf. When I hit a good shot, I want to remember what I did. I want to remember what I did to make the ball go that way. It does not happen all the time. When I hit the ball right, I want to remember what that felt like. That is what we try to teach in doing this drill. We want the blocker to feel the perfect position for the basic block.

From the fitted position, we go to the second phase called the *walk*. The blocker starts to walk the defender back by scooting his feet along the ground. The emphasis in this phase is the position of the head and back. We do not want the head down or into the chest of the defender. We want to keep the tail down and the back straight. We want the arch in the back and the hips down.

That was what Paul Alexander was talking about last night. When you get a player that can do this drill properly, that is the player you want to work with. You want to work with him and get him to the point where it is a constant process for him. The blocker on the walk maintains the arch in his back. His hips are on a rail, and he does not rise as he takes the defender back. He wants to use his hands to push the defender as he walks him. He works his feet in a straight line with his weight on the inside of his feet and his knees inside his body.

The third phase of the drill is to use the arms to get the defender away from the blocker (Diagram #4). From the fitted position, the blocker bench presses the defender away from him while simultaneously rolling his hips and thrusting his head up. If you do this on a sled, the blocker ends up in the belly-flop position on the ground. The blocker presses, hip rolls, and thrusts his head up to get movement on the defender backward. After we achieve the movement in the defender, the blocker gets back down and continues to drive.

Diagram #4. Hip Roll

When the blocker dips back down after the thrust, we call that "getting another bite." The blocker dips back down into his football position and continues to keep control of the defender. The fourth phase of the drill is to put all the movements together from the stance. The blocker gets into the stance. He explodes, punches his hands into the chest, presses with the arms, rolls the hips, thrusts the head up, achieves movement, and gets another bite as he moves the defender back. That is the block progression.

We want the linemen to understand this is a technical exercise. You cannot simply tell the blocker to knock the crap out of the defender. You have to teach him the steps to make it happen. Someone might have a different way to teach this skill. This is the way I teach it. There are a thousand ways to skin a cat. The block progression was something I did every day. I did it from the first day of training camp to the Friday before the last game of the season. I wanted that engrained in their minds of how to do things. When you engrain something and make it a habit, that is what they learn to do automatically. It becomes second nature to them.

What we are doing as offensive line coaches is teaching unnatural stuff. I do a bag and board drill every day. My favorite drill is chute, bag, and board. You put the blocker under the chute with the bag and board on the other side of the chute. The lineman fires through the chute, contacts the bag, and drives it down the board. He uses the techniques I just talked about in the block progression. He strikes the bag, presses, rolls his hips, gets another bite, and drives the bag the length of the board. That drill is as old as football itself.

I want to tell you a funny story. I was coaching at Carolina in 2003. If you have a good running back, you ride his butt. We had a great tailback by the name of Stephen Davis. In 2003, we ran a lot of power plays. Stephen Davis was uncanny at running this play. He could take the play inside, outside, or backside. By midseason, Carolina was close to leading the league in rushing. Carolina was never ranked that high in rushing the football.

Everyone in the league and around town thought we had a great offensive line. That was not the case. I will take an average offensive line and a great running back every time. If you have a great offensive line and an average running back, you are in trouble. The running back is the player that makes the play go.

We were rushing the ball to the tune of 165 to 170 yards a game. I had this writer come up to me and tell me he had been watching practice. He noticed we did the bag and board drills every day. He asked me if I invented the drill. I laughed and told him that drill was as old as the game itself. The first offensive line coach in history, whoever he may have been, put his players in a situation where they had to come out and not up.

That is how important those drills are because they teach your players to come off the ball low and not up in their charge. We do not want our players coming off the ball in an up position. We want them coming out and up and rolling their hips on contact. The power in the block is created from the hip girdle as the blocker rolls his hips and drives the defender back.

When I do the chute, bag, and board, I start with the blockers in the chute. I put them midway through the chute. The board is extended into the chute so that the blocker has to keep his feet apart from the get-go. I do not make them run through the entire width of the chute. I start them in the chute so the trajectory of their charge is the same angle they have to execute in a game. If they have to waddle under the width of the chute, it is not a natural movement. It does not assimilate the movement they have to perform in the game. The bags are placed directly in front of the blocker on the board.

In the drill, the linemen practice taking off with the right foot as well as the left foot. In today's football, the linemen align in a left-handed stance on the left side of the ball and a right-handed stance on the right side of the ball. They do not step with the same foot every time. They have to practice moving both feet from the same stance. You have to constantly work with your players going both ways from their stance.

The other bag and board drill I like to do is the T-board drill (Diagram #5). I am sure you coaches have all done that drill. I am not telling you something that you do not already know. I am telling you that you have to do the drills religiously. You cannot do these drills once a month. You have to do them every week. If you have three days of practice, try to do three bag drills and three board drills a week. Do the drills so your linemen are constantly working on the small individual techniques striving to get better.

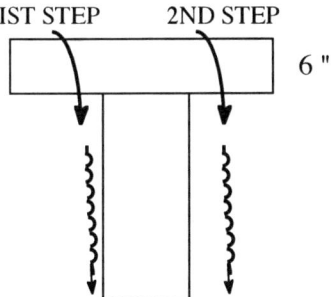

Diagram #5. T-Board

The T-boards are six-inch boards. When your players do this drill, make them put their feet against the T. When players do this drill, they want to get away from the board. They want to put one hand on the long board and get away from the T-board. They want to be able to step over the T-board and not take a short step to get there. Push them up and make them put their toes against the T. Make them feel uncomfortable so they have to do something that makes it feel unnatural. That makes them step with the first step over the T and forces them to get the second step over the T and on the ground quickly.

We do not want a long step over the T-board because you cannot get the second step back on the ground before the contact. If the offensive lineman takes on the defender with one foot on the ground, he loses. The defender will never take on the offensive blocker with one foot on the ground and one off the ground. The key to blocking is getting the second step down and fast as you can. I think the T-board is the thing that creates that aspect in the player's mind.

The contact comes on the second step. The block progression begins on the second step. The important thing to remember is to roll the hips to get movement, but you cannot maintain that position. Once the blocker gets movement, he has to get his hips back down and drive. He has to get another bite. The T-board is no different than the chute/board drill. The offensive linemen have to step with both feet. They step with the right foot first, and the next time, they step with the left foot first. You cannot allow your players to step with the same foot all the time.

The third board drill is the angled-board drill (Diagram #6). The boards are placed at a 45-degree angle to the offensive linemen. This works the offensive linemen on their lateral-lead steps or drop-steps. They take a lateral-lead step, attack the bag on their second step, and drive the bag down the board. This assimilates the block on a 3 technique or 5 technique on the guard and tackle or a shade technique for the center. The center has to work the drill both ways.

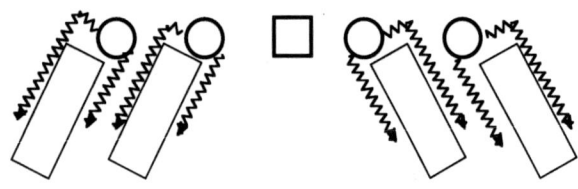

Diagram #6. Angled-Board

This is not a reach-block drill. The blocker wants to drive the bag down the board. We want the target on this type of block on the midline of the defender. We want to drive the defender back on an angle, not a hook block or scramble block. That is what I used to do in college. I could not knock people off the ball, but I could scramble block. That is why I got to play. The aim point on the defender is important. If the defender is head-up the blocker, his aiming point is slightly off the midline to the side we want to drive the defender.

I like to do movement drills with the offensive line. One of my favorite drills to do was a *gather drill* (Diagram #7). The players hated the drill, so I knew it

was a good drill. I used three half-round dummies. The players had to pull and run over the dummies. There was a defender with a bag five yards outside the last dummy. After the blocker crossed the last bag, he had to gather his momentum in space. The defender with the dummy ran up or down the field. The blocker had to drop his hips and chase him. This was a great drill for guards versus linebackers. We also pulled the tackles and centers, and this drill helped them blocking in space.

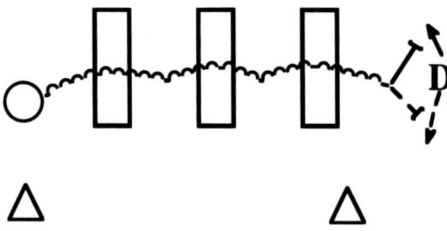

Diagram #7. Gather Drill

When the defender moves, the offensive blocker has to get into position to block the guy. He has to gather himself and get his center of gravity back between his feet and over his knees so he can move one way or another.

I did another drill similar to that drill, which went along with the block progression drill. I put the blocker in the fitted block progression drill. When I said, "Go," the blocker went through his block progression. When I said, "Go" the second time, the defender tried to run away from the blocker. The blocker had to finish the block and chase the defender.

I was talking to Bob before I came up, and we talked about the *zigzag drill* that Cincinnati used. It was a mirror-type drill for the offensive blocker. The blocker locked up on the defender in a fit position. The defender moved from side to side in a zigzag motion. The blocker had to keep contact and position on the defender as he moved.

Any drill you can do where a blocker has to control his body is a good movement drill. That type of skill is most important for an offensive lineman. When I look at players on tape, that is one of the things I look for. He might be big, strong, fast, quick, and tough, but if he cannot control his body, he cannot play. If he looks like he is falling out of a four-story building all the time, he cannot play.

In doing the drill, we are trying to create unnatural situations so they can get better at what they do. I love sled drills. As I told you in the hip-roll drill, it is a belly-flop drill on the sled. We did that drill from a six-point stance. We did the hip roll drill with the hands, knees, and toes in the ground. When I was at Boston College, I always did a sled progression. We did a right shoulder and left shoulder drill. We did the block progression while driving the sled. Sled drills are important teachers of coming off the ball.

I always told our players that the sled was their friend—a Crowther or Rogers sled was their friend—and they needed to work with him every day. The drills you use should work along with the particular concept or scheme you are working that day or week. It does not matter whether it is zone blocking, trap blocking, gap blocking, or whatever you are teaching that particular week. The drills must accomplish that particular skill.

The mistake we make in the block progression is in the finish of the block. We press the defender, roll the hips, and thrust the head up, but we do not finish the block by getting the hips back down. You cannot continue to get movement from a locked-out position. You have to reestablish your low position to finish the block. I have to continually coach my players to get them down. They think since they have the defender stalemated that their job is over. Eventually, the defender will shed the offensive blocker and make the play. In order to finish, the blocker has to be in position to finish.

Everything we do in zone blocking is developed off the lateral-lead step. All the offensive linemen at the point of attack are in concert with their footwork. If I am the right guard and I'm working with the center on a zone combination block, our footwork has to match. If our block is a combination block for the shade nose and the backside linebacker, the footwork has to be together. The right guard and center use a lateral-lead step, and they work off the ball at the same angle and direction. Depending on which way the shade nose goes determines the blocker that blocks the backside linebacker.

The linemen have to get their shoulders in the proper position. If we run the inside zone play, the shoulder tilt and angle of the lateral-lead step is more vertical in the charge. If the zone is an outside zone, the lateral-lead step is more horizontal in nature. The shoulders will be turned more to the line of scrimmage because of the width of the play.

When we look at tape of our linemen, we evaluate them by their footwork and angles. We look to see if their shoulders are in the proper position. We look to see if they are stepping with the proper foot and getting the proper footwork. Zone blocking became an inside or outside process. There were two sides to the concepts. The frontside was the point of attack, and the backside was dealing with creating the cutback lanes.

The backside blockers are trying to get vertical push up the field. They work to get vertical push keeping their shoulders square. The tackle and backside guard may be working on the 3 technique in the same fashion as the center and frontside guard on the shade nose. They are trying to create a situation where the running back can get underneath the tackle's block on the backside. The frontside linemen are trying to cover up the defenders. They have to cover up the defenders, but they must come off the ball properly with their shoulders at the proper angle. They cannot come off the ball having already rolled their hips because they cannot generate any power to get the movement, which is necessary on the zone play.

When we run the outside zone, we have a different mind-set. The angles for the frontside player become flatter to the outside, and we want to create rapid movement to the outside. The aiming point for the blocks is wider, and we want to stretch the defenders to the outside. On the backside, we want to cut down the defender. If we can accomplish that to the backside, we can separate the defense.

The Denver Broncos are a perfect example of that concept. They want to separate the frontside from the backside. The way they do it is the chop block or cut block. I see nothing wrong with a chop or cut block. The only time I do is when the offensive blocker hits the defender from behind when they are at the same level. The correct way to perform this block is with the head in front of the defender. The chop block does not occur in the first step.

If the backside tackle is going to cut the 3-technique defender, he takes a drop-step to get off the line of scrimmage. He turns and runs on the proper angle down the line of scrimmage. On the third or fourth step, he gets his head across the defender and cuts his playside knee. If he is slightly ahead of the defender, he can get the cut block.

What I do not want the blocker to do is clip the defender. If the tackle is going to cut the 3-technique defender, he has to get ahead of him. If the defender has gotten penetration to the same level as the tackle, I do not want the tackle to throw on the defender in the back of his legs. That is not right, and it is not what that block is all about. There are people that teach it differently and cut regardless of the situation.

When I was with Jacksonville, we had Fred Taylor and ran exclusively the inside and outside zone play. We lead the league one year, and our best play was the stretch play. Fred took the ball wide and cut it back because we separated the defense with our cut blocking. If the backside tried to throw too quickly, the defenders played off the cut block. The offensive blocker had to work his way down the line of scrimmage to get into position before he threw.

This block is another example of an unnatural act. The more you rep and drill those skills, the better you become at them. This attitude has to be a way of life. The offensive linemen complain all the time about doing the same things repeatedly. However, in the long run that is what makes them better.

Question: How do you teach the cut block in practice?

When we drill the cut block, we use dummies. The dummy holder uses a tube dummy. On the snap of the ball, he moves down the line of scrimmage a couple of steps with the dummy. The cut blocker takes his drop-step, gets on the proper angle, and on the second or third step, he fires his backside flipper and forearm through the dummy. When we work against the scouts, we use a different technique. I got this from Alex Gibbs. We do not want to cut the scout team. On the snap of the ball, the tackle takes his drop-step, comes down the line of scrimmage, and grabs the defender instead of cutting him. The defenders do not particularly like it, but at least we do not cut them and it serves the same purpose.

When I was at Carolina, we ran what I called a rap draw. We ran two types of draws. We ran a lead draw and a rap draw. On the lead draw, we doubled the nose tackle to the backside linebacker. We isolated with the fullback on the Mike linebacker (Diagram #8). The strongside tackle and tight end base blocked on the tackle and outside linebacker. To the backside, we fan blocked the guard and tackle to that side.

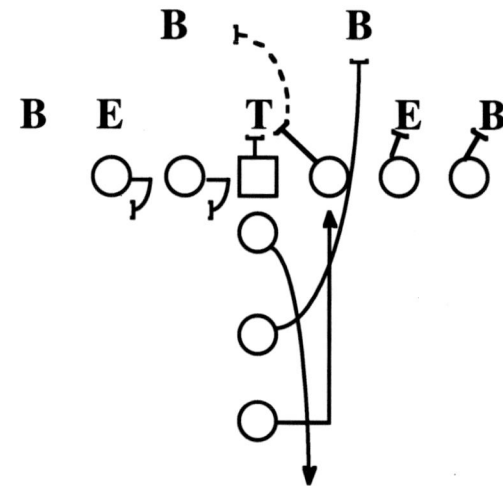

Diagram #8. Lead Draw

If we ran the lead draw to the backside, we ran it the same way except the strongside guard and center combined on the nose and Mike linebacker.

The play we got a ton of yardage on was the rap draw (Diagram #9). We blocked it the same way as the lead draw to the weakside. The difference in the play was the path of the fullback and tailback. We took the fullback and started him to the strongside. He wrapped his path around the quarterback to isolate the backside linebacker. The tailback took the same path. It looked like a counter draw off the lead draw.

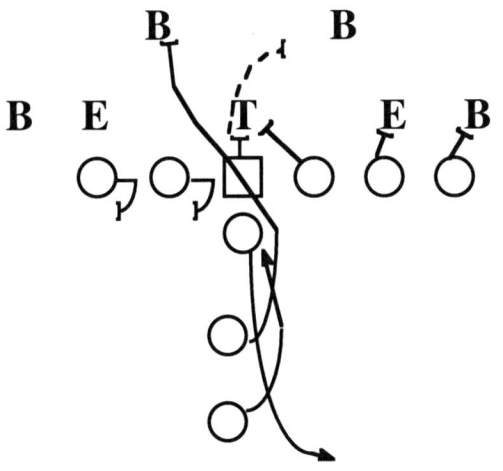

Diagram #9. Rap Draw

The key factor to the play is the backside 3-technique defender. The backside guard has to make the defender do something. He cannot let the defender stay on the line of scrimmage and chicken fight with him. The guard has got to make the defender commit one way or the other. If he goes inside, the guard flattens him out and drives him down the line of scrimmage. If he charges up the field outside, the guard drives him upfield. If the defender does nothing, the guard has to drive block him off his spot.

The callside guard on a draw play has to move his defender off that spot. He has to create a seam or space for the ball to be run into. The backside guard and center have to drive the nose off the line of scrimmage to linebacker depth and get off on the linebacker. Hopefully, the linebacker reads the play as pass and drops.

If the center pops up on the nose as if it were a pass before he gets into the block, it will be a better play. The backside guard can show pass to influence the linebacker before he gets involved with the

center on the nose. The guard cannot get on the nose right away or the linebacker will read draw immediately. The guard has to create some space by giving the linebacker the illusion it is a pass. The callside tackle shows pass and takes the defensive end outside. We ran this play a lot when we had Stephen Davis. He was a great running back and could find the crease and spot every time. He could read, react, and get through cracks in the defense.

I worked for John Fox at Carolina. He is a defensive coach. John made the statement that the biggest mismatch in sports was an NFL offensive lineman versus an NFL defensive lineman. From an athletic standpoint, I agree with him. However, I do not agree with him from a mental standpoint. I could fall out of bed and coach the defensive line. All you have to do is: see the ball, find the ball, and get the ball. Coaching the offensive line is a tough way to make a living. We work with less athletic players in difficult situations. However, after it is all said and done, I would not want to coach another position. I love being with those players.

They have a great sense of humor, a great outlook on life, and they work their butts off. As Jack Bicknell said, "They will be successful. They would work for nothing. They understand the big picture and know they have to work at their position to be successful. They know it will not come easy to them."

If we got an over defense, we still ran the rap draw (Diagram #10). The tight end worked up the field at the Sam linebacker. The backside tackle stepped out on the defensive end. The guard based the 3 technique. The callside guard and center combo blocked on the nose to the Mike linebacker. The callside tackle stepped out on the defensive end to his side. The fullback and tailback read the combo block of the center and guard and ran off that block. The fullback and tailback started to the strongside and wrapped the play to the weakside of the formation.

If we did not combo on the nose, we schemed him. We could block down on him with the guard and pull the center around for the Mike linebacker. It is a

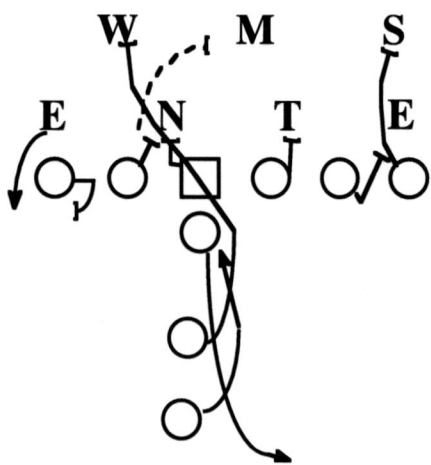

Diagram #10. Rap Draw vs. Under

simple play and it is a counter draw. We always look for plays that are counter or misdirection plays. Offensive linemen like counter plays—they are the types of plays where you can get the defensive lineman looking one way and the offensive lineman gets to earhole him.

I talked to Bob Wylie before I came and asked him what topic he wanted me to cover today. He said since I was with the Dolphins last year, it might be nice to talk about the Wildcat formation (Diagram #11). I felt kind of funny because I have never been a big X's and O's type of coach. I have always talked about fundamentals. In the Wildcat, we aligned in an unbalanced set at the line of scrimmage. The quarterback aligned at the wide receiver on the line of scrimmage to the three-man surface.

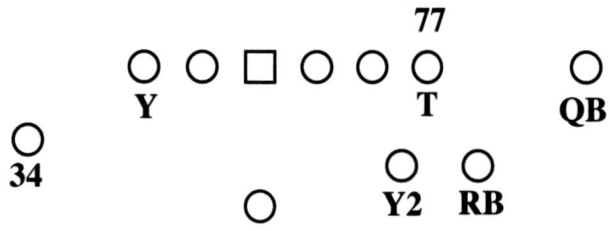

Diagram #11. Wildcat

The tight end position to the unbalanced side was Jake Long, an offensive tackle. The first tight end aligned as an eligible receiver on the end of the two-man side. Ricky Williams, number 34, aligned as the split receiver to the two-man side. Ronnie

Brown, number 23, aligned in the shotgun set behind the center, and the second tight end aligned in the gap between the two tackles. The extra running back aligned in the wide slot to the unbalanced side. We played with two tight ends, three running backs, and no wide receivers. The whole thing about this kind of stuff is you never know what you are going to get from the defense.

I would go crazy on Tuesday. We sat in the meeting room and argued about what we were going to do with this set. We talked about all these different things that I had to make happen. I had five players I had to coach to make these things happen. The rest of the coaches have maybe one or, at the most, two players to coach. I did not have the brightest bulbs in the world playing for me. The whole deal was how the defense was going to adjust to the unbalanced set. They had to adjust either the front or the secondary. What I had to do was prepare for what the defense was going to do.

When we played New England, they moved the defensive front over one man (Diagram #12). They played a 3-4 defense. The nose moved over the strong guard. The backside end and outside linebacker reduced down to the two-man side. The backside inside linebacker moved over the center, and the strongside linebacker bumped into a 50 alignment on the inside tackles. The first thing we decided to run was power.

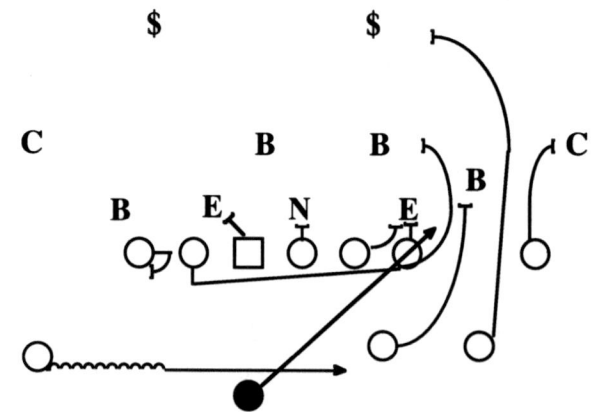

Diagram #12. Power vs. 3-4 Adjustment

On the power, we double-teamed the defensive end with the two tackles working for the backside linebacker. The strongside guard base blocked the 2-technique defender covering him. The second tight end in the backfield blocked the outside linebacker. The center blocked back for the pulling guard. The backside guard pulled around the double-team and picked up the first linebacker to show. The backside tight end pass blocked the outside linebacker to his side. The running back in the slot to the wideside blocked the first thing to show off the edge.

The quarterback got in the way of the corner and tried not to get hurt. Ricky Williams came in motion toward the Wildcat. Ronnie Brown took the shotgun snap, faked to Ricky, and ran the ball off the double-team to the strongside. We ran the power play six times and gained 130 yards. It was a hot offense after that game. The offense is all right as long as the defense does exactly what we think they will do.

The next week we played San Diego. Luckily, they were a 3-4 defensive team. However, they did not play the Wildcat the same way Belichick played it. The first series after we ran the Wildcat, I was on the sideline trying to put out the fires. I was going crazy on the sideline trying to figure out who was supposed to block whom. You are trying to teach a basic concept, but you do not know what the defense is going to do. That makes it different.

Another base play out of the Wildcat is the outside zone (Diagram #13). We ran Ricky Williams in motion and gave the ball to him. Ronnie Brown faked the ball out the backside on the naked bootleg. The slot running back came up the field and blocked outside the outside linebacker. The two tackles zone combo on the defensive end with one of them coming off for the linebacker. The backside, center, and callside guard zone blocked to the unbalanced side. The second tight end captured the edge, and we had Ricky Williams on the outside zone play in space.

We let the backside outside linebacker, corner, and safety run free. We did not block them. We ran the zone concept and blocked whatever we saw. We gave the two tackles a basic rule. If one of them was covered and the other was uncovered, they

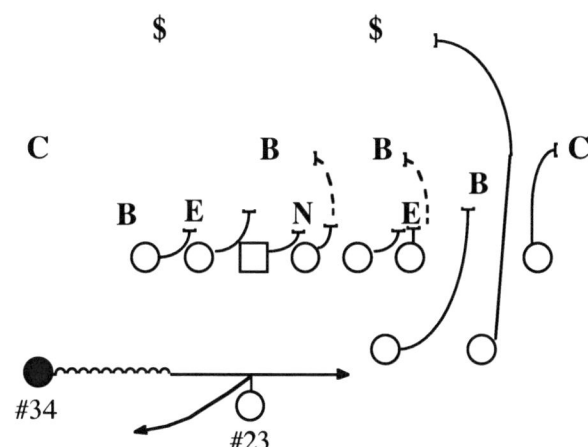

Diagram #13. Wildcat Outside Zone

zone blocked together. The outside tackle always tried to capture the edge.

The third play in the Wildcat took advantage of teams that tried to support with the strong safety to the side of the unbalanced set (Diagram #14). This is the play we ran against Houston. They decided they would bring the strong safety down to the side of the unbalanced set. We ran the outside zone play to Ricky Williams and blocked it the same way. The slot running back took the safety coming down for support. He blocked him and then slipped down the middle of the field. The quarterback aligned at the wide receiver. He faked down the field and retreated back toward Ricky Williams who was running the outside zone play.

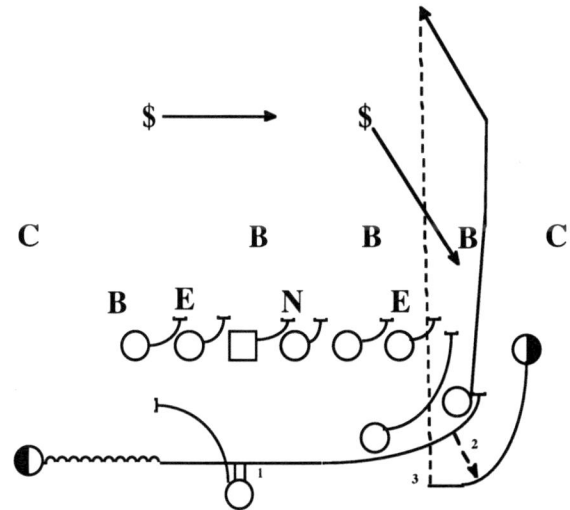

Diagram #14. Wildcat Outside Zone Pass

Ricky Williams pitched the ball to the quarterback and blocked anything coming to the quarterback. The quarterback took the pitch and threw to the running back down the middle of the football field. Ronnie Brown who handed the ball to Ricky Williams secured the backside of the play. We hit that play for 80 yards against Houston.

We ran the naked bootleg off the zone fake (Diagram #15). We ran the zone play fake to Ricky Williams. Ronnie faked the ball to Ricky and ran the naked bootleg out the backside. The tight end to the two-man side blocked down and then released to the flat. The second tight end in the backfield released through the line and ran a drag pattern off the backside of the play. It is a basic play except we were unbalanced and did not have a quarterback.

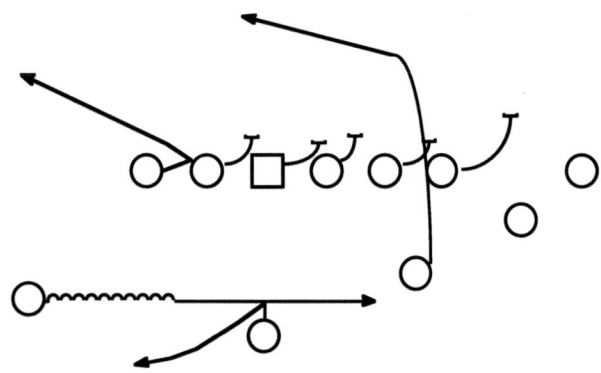

Diagram #15. Wildcat Naked Bootleg

The offense is a single-wing concept. The quarterback called the play, but he did not get the ball. The tailback received the direct snap. We spent Tuesdays trying to come up with something different for the Wildcat offense. We wanted to be able to change things up. We would run the Wildcat personnel on the field and run a normal play with them. We did that to keep the defensive coordinator from matching personnel with the Wildcat personnel. That allowed us to run the Wildcat personnel on the field but not run a Wildcat play.

Miami drafted Pat White from West Virginia. With that player, they can put him into the position where Ronnie Brown played and have a real threat to throw the ball on any play. He can run and throw, and he throws the ball very well.

I have to give Dan Henning credit. He is a smart guy and he will come up with something. The Wildcat for us was nothing more than a gimmick situation. We were 0-2 coming back from Arizona where we got our butts handed to us. We could not create any space in our running attack. We used the Wildcat to try and create some space for our running backs.

If I have left you with anything, I am hoping I left you with the idea that fundamentals are what the offensive line is about. You are dealing with fundamentals all the time and adjusting them to your players. You constantly drill them with repetition because they are unnatural acts. The more you drill them and work at them, the better you become. It is a constant process of making them believe they can get better at what they are doing.

Your job is tough. I know for many years at Boston College, we had players who passed the "look test" but would not hit anyone. We had to make those players tough. The way we did that was to throw them in with the veterans who had been in the program. Those players will make the younger players tough, or they will leave the program. It is the old statement, "Go hard or go home." I was at BC for 13 years. I could tell you story upon story of guys in that program. High school All-Americans came in that we had to literally start from scratch with in relationship to their skills. Of course, there were also the other players who came in from a high school program and could contribute right off the bat.

Gentlemen, I hope I left you with something and I appreciate your time.

ABOUT THE AUTHOR

Mike Maser spent the 2008 season as the offensive line coach for the Miami Dolphins. He came to the Dolphins with 35 years of coaching experience, including 13 as an offensive line coach in the National Football League.

Prior to joining the Dolphins, Maser was an offensive line coach with the Carolina Panthers from 2003 to 2006. During that span, the Panthers compiled a regular-season record of 37-27 and made two trips to the NFC Championship game (2003 and 2005) and appeared in Super Bowl XXXVIII. Under Maser, the Panthers' offensive line consistently ranked among the league's best. During Maser's tenure with the team, tackle Jordan Gross was an all-rookie selection in 2003 while guard Mike Wahle was chosen for the Pro Bowl in 2005. The Panthers' offensive line allowed only 119 sacks under Maser, which represents the sixth-best figure in the NFL and was second among NFC clubs during that four-year span. In 2003, Carolina rushed for 2,091 yards and allowed only 26 sacks, still the best figures in franchise history in their respective categories.

Prior to joining the Panthers, Maser held the same position with the Jacksonville Jaguars from 1994 to 2002, having joined the expansion franchise one year prior to its inaugural season of 1995. While there, the club reached the AFC Championship game in just its second year of existence—one which began a stretch of four straight winning seasons, including a pair of AFC Central Division titles. In Jacksonville, Maser led an offensive line that continually helped the team's running game to rank among the best in the NFL. The team ran for more than 2,000 yards in four of Maser's final five seasons with the club, including a then-franchise record 2,102 yards in 1998, a mark that stood until the 2006 campaign. The 2,091 rushing yards the Jaguars amassed in 1999 was the second-best mark in the league that season, and the Jaguars were the only NFL franchise to top the 2,000-yard rushing barrier each season from 1998 to 2000. Maser's offensive lines also demonstrated a knack for helping ballcarriers find the end zone, as the Jaguars' 107 rushing touchdowns from 1997 to 2002 led the league.

With the Jaguars, Maser developed left tackle Tony Boselli, who was selected to the Pro Bowl every season from 1996 to 2000 and was joined there in 1999 by right tackle Leon Searcy. In addition, Maser tutored three players who became all-rookie selections in center Michael Cheever (1996), guard Brad Meester (2000), and tackle Maurice Williams (2001).

Before joining the NFL coaching ranks, Maser spent 22 seasons at the collegiate level, including the fi-nal 13 as offensive line coach at Boston College (1981 to 1993), during which time he worked under both Jack Bicknell (1981 to 1990) and Tom Coughlin (1991 to 1993). Maser helped the Eagles reach six bowl games following a period in which the team had gone 40 years without making a bowl appearance. Maser's offensive line protected Boston College quarterback Doug Flutie during the 1984 season when he became the first and only Heisman Trophy winner in school history. During Maser's tenure at Boston College, 10 of his pupils along the line went on to play in the NFL.

A native of Clayton, New York, Maser was a three-year starter at guard at the University of Buffalo (1966 to 1968) and helped the Bulls to a record of 7-3 during his senior season before graduating with a degree in health, physical education, and recreation. He earned his master's degree in physical education from Marshall University. Maser and his wife, Barbara, have three grown children.

MASER AT A GLANCE

- 2008: Miami Dolphins, Offensive Line Coach
- 2003-2006: Carolina Panthers, Offensive Line Coach
- 1994-2002: Jacksonville Jaguars, Offensive Line Coach
- 1981-1993: Boston College, Offensive Line Coach
- 1979-1980: Maine, Offensive Line Coach
- 1974-1978: Bluefield State College, Offensive Line Coach
- 1973: Marshall University, Offensive Line Coach

NEW THINGS YOU SHOULD KNOW THAT WORK

Retired NFL Offensive Line Coach

Thank you, Bob Wylie. We started these clinics in 1984. We had about 10 coaches show up and I charged $10 a coach. It is a pleasure to be here. I really cannot tell you a lot because everyone has covered everything I know. I worked for the Bengals for 15 years. I am close to the University of Cincinnati, and I do some things for them. However, I actually have an office at the University at Buffalo, where I went to college.

I played football there, believe it or not. However, I was 40 pounds heavier than I am now, and you did not have to be 6'4" to play in my day. I am a volunteer for the University at Buffalo. We won the Mid-American conference last year and played in a bowl game. We lost to Connecticut. Turner Gill has done a fantastic job there.

I have an office there but the compliance people are on me heavy so I do not do much. I go to high schools and colleges, and I talk to some pro coaches and people actually pay me. I used to do it for free. I go all over the country and talk about some things I think are important.

I want to tell you there are a million ways to get it done. No one has the exact answer. We have vision and goals, and we think our way is the only way to do things. But trust me, as long as you are out there coaching and getting results, your way is the best way. If you do not know something, you have to find out.

I have learned one thing, and I hope you coaches are not where I was. When I was coaching, I coached in some situations where the team did not do so well. I could not wait for the time when some of my best friends got the crap kicked out of them so they would know how I felt. When someone gets a lot of credit, you cannot wait to see them get their butts kicked. When you get to the point where you are rooting for your buddy, then you know you have made it as a coach.

We all have those big egos. After a year and a half out of the competitive coaching business, I do not feel that way anymore. I hope everyone does well, and I believe we all know what we are doing. I want to go over some things that I have done in my career or things I have learned.

I am not going to say I invented the Duck Demeanor drill, but I almost did. Everyone in the country does that drill now. When I was at Wake Forest University in 1978, there was a coach by the name of Ernie Zwahlen who coached for the Baltimore Colts. I went up to see him. He was doing this drill where he had the players doing real mechanical duck steps in a football position. He had them in a low position but not down into the duckwalk position.

DUCK DEMEANOR DRILL

- Get into a stance with the feet slightly wider than shoulder-width apart.
- Drop down like a linebacker with chest over knees; weight on balls of the feet.

Coach's Directions

- Right and left movement. When going right/left, the player will always lead-step and slide the back foot.
- Shuffle (the right foot moves six inches and the left foot moves six inches).
- Carry hands high in front of the face and look ready to strike a punch.

- When moving backward/forward, steps are power steps in duck-like fashion.
- Keep elbows tucked to the rib cage, pumping hands and arms in running form.
- Keep feet close to the ground. Always keep a good base, and do not let the feet click together.

I took that drill and everywhere I went, I added something to it. This is the only agility drill I do. I do not use bags, chutes, or boards. I am not saying I am right, but this is the only drill I use. When you do the drill, the feet are slightly wider than the shoulders. The knees are bent and over the toes. The foot hits flat on the ground when they do the movement. We incorporate the hands and feet together. We want to go fast with the hands and feet. We do the movement forward using the duck step and rapid arm and hand movement. We never want to step forward where the foot crosses over itself. The feet stay in perfect alignment and never cross over on any step.

After we go straight forward, I give them a direction to step. To keep the drill going with the proper duck step, they cannot lead step to the direction I point. If they do, their second step narrows their base. They must drop step with the foot to the side they are going. By using the drop-step, it opens the hips and allows them to get the whole foot on the ground. The second step keeps the wide base and allows them to duck step on an angle.

I move them forward, backward, and on an angle. The next movement is side to side like a pass-pro movement. When we do the side-to-side movement, we never want the feet to drag on the ground. We want to step with the feet and not slide them on the ground. By staying in the football position using the duck steps, they go forward, backward, on an angle, and side to side, always keeping the wide base.

We do a drill with two players. The blocker moves in the direction the opposite player sends him. He points right, left, forward, backward, and on the angle. At some point in the drill, the opposite player charges the blocker. The blocker forearms

him or pass blocks the player, but the drill is to keep the feet going throughout the entire drill.

The problem with the bags and shields that most of us use is that there is nothing to grab. When the blocker hits the flat shield, he has nothing to grab onto. When you are blocking, you want to be able to grab things in your hands.

The other thing is that defensive players never give the offensive blocker a look. When you do board and chute drills, the blocker comes out, hits the bag, and drives it down the board. The defender holding the bag backs up, and the blocker is constantly chasing the bag down the board. The defensive player should be a stone wall. If you are running a stretch play and blocking a 3 technique, you should hit and work down the line of scrimmage. When the blocker hits the bag, he is chasing it every time.

That is not what happens in a game. When the offensive blocker hits the defender, there is a stalemate almost every time. If you are going to use bags, the defensive players must give more resistance for the drill to mimic game-like situations.

In the old days, when we blocked on an angle, we used a lead step. The problem with that is the second step. If you lead step at the defender, the second step crosses over itself and you end up with a narrow base. The whole idea is to get the lead foot out of the way so you can get the second foot on the ground. The whole concept of all the blocking I have ever done is how fast I can get the lead step out of the way so I can get the second step on the ground.

If I am blocking on an angle to the right side, the right foot is dropped off the line of scrimmage six inches and braced on the ground (Diagram #1). The whole foot is on the ground at an angle to the outside. That allows the second step to move quickly back to the ground without crossing over itself. You use the step in the duck demeanor drill. The steps allow the first foot to get out of the way and the second foot to get back to the ground while maintaining a wide base.

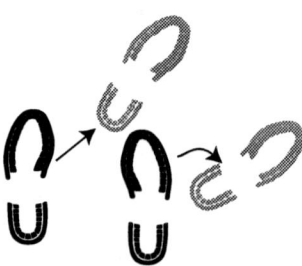

Diagram #1. Brace Step

That means the blocker is blocking on an angle. The blocker wants to get the lead foot out of the way and step with the second foot so he can block the defender on the angle he is on. The ball is going that way, and I want to block the defender that way. He is not trying to slide over and get square on the defender or step at an angle with his lead foot. Even if the defender aligned head-up the blocker, I would use the same footwork. I would drop the first foot into the brace step and attack with the second step.

When you are blocking, I think you should always take two steps before contact. You never want to try and block when you take one step and make contact with the defender. When you take two steps, it lowers the center of gravity. When you take the brace step, it lowers the butt and loads the second step to the contact. By taking the brace step, you coil the momentum on the second step. On the third step, you uncoil off the back foot. To initiate a block, you have to move the feet two times.

The knees control the weight shift in the stance. If the guard wants to go to his right, he puts weight on his left knee. He pivots down on the left knee, and that puts the weight on the left cheek of his butt. That takes it off the right side so he can move the right foot. If the blocker wants to pass block or run block to his right, he drives the left knee down to shift the weight off the right side.

When the offensive lineman comes off the ball to block, and particularly a linebacker, he has to gather himself before the block. If he has to block a linebacker, he cannot simply fly off the ball and expect to get a hit on him. As he approaches the linebacker, he has to gather his feet and get them on the ground before he strikes the linebacker. We talked earlier about the quick-foot duck step. That keeps you from getting out of control and missing completely.

When the lineman is blocking, he is always fighting his own force. He is trying to go forward hard, but there is something that has to pull him back. If the blocker flies off the ball, he is out of control. When the lineman comes out of his stance, the movement is like the upper body going forward but the lower body catches and holds the blocker back. That allows the blocker to pick up a slant by the defender. It allows him to adjust to movement by the defender. The blocker's upper body is forward, but his footwork gathers and keeps him under control.

If the blocker has no help inside, he has to stay with a slanting lineman and has to be under control to stay with him. If he has help inside as in the zone scheme, he can be more aggressive off the ball. The worst thing he can do is get overextended. If he gets overextended, his second step will be too long. The only time overextending does not hurt is on the goal line. You are not standing up, but you are not coming off so hard that you cannot get your second step down.

The next thing I want to show you is something that is kind of new but it is natural. When the blocker hits a defender on the line, there are two things that are going to happen. When the blocker hits the defender, he is going to knock him back a little or the defender moves so the lineman has to chase him. The other thing that could occur is the defender stalemates the blocker.

I see everyone in football blocking with their arms in a locked-out position, pushing on the defender. That may be fine if you have to catch a defender that is running away from the block. You do not want to push the defender away from you with your arms locked out. You want to grab his arms and lift him. You want to roll your hips into the defender's hips and lift him with the arms. You want to climb up his front side. That gets the lineman's feet out of the hole so the back can see the crease.

This type of movement is called a *double under* (Diagram #2). The blocker does not wind up with his arms as he comes off. He snaps the hands up and into the hands of the defender. The defender will try to punch the blocker in the breastplate with his hand. When the defender extends his hand toward the blocker, the blocker explodes with his hands, grabs the defender's hands, and drives the defender's hands and arms up. At the same time, he gets into the defender's body by rolling his hip into the defender's hips and climbing up his frame.

Diagram #2. Double Under

The blocker has to leverage the defender and get under him. He keeps his knees bent and works the feet as he impacts the hands. The defender's hands are coming straight for the blocker's chest. He has 300 pounds of force directed at the chest of the blocker. Using the double under, the blocker redirects the force of the defender coming forward to an upward direction by punching up with his hands and lifting with his arms. If the blocker tries to press the defender off his body, he is pushing against the force of the defender. That leads to a stalemate. The thing to remember is not to extend with the knees but to lift with the arms.

You can do the same thing by grabbing the belt or getting under the cantilever of the shoulder pads. You want to grab on to something and lift with the arms while keeping the knees bent. In this type of movement, you can roll the hips while keeping the knees bent. The bent knee is what gives the blocker power. When you extend the arms, that is the way to get your feet out of the hole and blunt the force of the defender. The head is not part of the block. The head barely comes in contact with the defender. The only thing the head does is to align the target area.

The head is relative to where the ball is being run. If the ball is going right, the head is placed to the right of the midline of the defender. The wider the ball is run, the wider the target on the defender.

On every block, the lineman has to have a *high knee*. If the right guard reaches for a 3-technique defender, his high knee is his inside knee. He does not want to have his feet parallel when he is trying to block. The inside leg should be ahead of the outside leg. Along with the high inside leg, the blocker wants to have a strong inside hand. He wants the inside leg up in the block and the inside hand to be strong on the defender. The softer hand goes with the leg that is back in the block.

If the ball is going outside of the lineman, the defender will try to move in that direction. The high inside leg allows the blocker to recover outside because his outside leg is back. The blocker keeps contact, pulls with his inside hand, and steps down the line with his outside leg. By using this technique, he can reset his helmet on the defender. The majority of the blocks a lineman makes are these types of blocks, and we do not practice them. The blocks are made going sideways. They are not made on a board blasting someone back 10 yards.

What happens on the zone play deals with the helmet placement. On the initial block, the lineman sets his helmet on the target. If the defender moves outside and the blocker does not reset his helmet, the running back will cut the ball back. By keeping the high inside leg and strong inside hand, as the defender moves to the outside, the blocker can move and reset his helmet. That gives the running back two more steps to the outside.

If we run the outside zone play, the lineman thinks he has to put his helmet in the outside armpit of the defender. If he tries to get his head in that position, the defender knocks him sideways and flats him to the line of scrimmage. The lineman does not have to get his helmet to the outside armpit coming off the ball. The running back does not have the ball when the blocker comes off the line. He can take the defender down the middle and reset his helmet as he gets into the block.

With the strong inside hand, the blocker wants to pull the defender to the hole. We want to create movement laterally in the defender as fast as we can. That makes the cutback lane wider. The strong inside hand lets the blocker throw the defender once he gets past his center of gravity. We do not want the defender falling back to the inside and making the tackle. As the defender gets past the blocker's center of gravity, the blocker pivots with his outside foot and shovels as hard as he can with the inside hand. That will twist the defender and throw him outside so he cannot recover to the inside.

In the zone play, the back is seven yards deep. You are better off if you define the aiming point for the running back as the inside leg of the guard, tackle, or end. When you declare these spots, the defense pursues differently than when you declare other spots. Running at the butt of the guard, to me, is not as good as running at the inside leg of the guard. When the back runs tighter, the linebackers do different things. The running back's keys are better.

If you have a zone play at the inside leg of the tackle and a stretch play at the inside leg of the tight end, you are wasting your time because they are the same play. You cannot tell if the running back is running at the inside leg of the tackle or the tight end. If the back runs slow enough, the defense moves so quickly you cannot tell what the play is. The inside zone play, to me, is the inside leg of the guard. Anything outside the inside leg of the guard is a stretch play.

On the inside zone, if the right guard has a 3 technique aligned on his outside shoulder, his helmet goes down the midline of the blocker. If the ball is going off the inside leg of the guard, the blocker gets up on the ball with his alignment. The defender is probably not going to move because the ball is coming inside the guard. However, if the defender moves outside, the blocker pivots on his outside foot and throws the defender outside.

If the ball is going outside of the guard, he gets off the ball a little farther and puts his helmet to the outside of the midline of the defender. However, if the ball is going wider, the footwork has to change. The first thing I do is get farther off the ball in my alignment. I do not want to use a wider brace step because the angle to the target is bad. The defender will flatten the blocker and may penetrate. The blocker uses a shuffle step before the brace step. He shuffles with his outside foot, his inside foot, drops the brace step, and gets the second foot down into the block.

Whenever you have to make up ground, you want to get off the ball and use small shuffle steps to widen the technique and get closer to the defender. We are still using all the techniques I have talked about. We still use the brace step, double under, high inside leg, and strong inside hand.

If the play is a wide play going around the end, the blocker gets a high outside leg. He uses his shuffle step as he does on the zone plays except he wants to get his outside leg high and his outside hand strong. He wants to seal the defender to the inside.

The finish to all these blocks is the climb, torque, or shove. If the defender is not moving to the outside, we climb him and get the feet out of the hole. If he is moving outside, we torque or throw him outside once the defender gets past the blocker's center of gravity.

Another way we use the shuffle step is to cut off the backside defenders. If the left guard has to cut off a 1-technique defender to his inside, he uses the shuffle step. He takes two shuffle steps with his inside and outside foot. He shuffles with his inside foot, then shuffles with his outside foot. After the shuffle, he brace steps and makes the block. He has moved laterally for two steps, which improves his angle and lets him cut off the defender without getting turned. When you have to make up distance on a defender, move laterally first. Another example is the backside tight end trying to cut off a 7-technique defender. He cannot block that defender unless he shuffles to improve his angle.

On the zone play, the toughest thing to block is the gray area (Diagram #3). If the onside tackle has a 5-technique defender aligned on him and he is working with the guard on that zone block, there is a gray area if the technique is not right. If the 5-technique defender goes straight ahead, there is a problem. The tackle uses his zone step and overreaches the defender. The guard uses his zone step and cannot reach the defender because he is too wide. The defender splits the zone combination block and gets penetration.

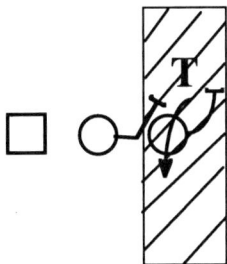

Diagram #3. Gray Area

If the defender reacts outside on the tackle's zone step or spikes inside, there is no problem. However, if he goes straight ahead, he works in the gray area of the two blocks. To avoid that problem, you need the offensive guard and tackle working in tandem with their butts together (Diagram #4). The guard has to take his shuffle steps to close the space between himself and the defender. He takes the shuffle steps and then takes his brace step and gets into his zone block. That allows him to overtake the block on the defender over the tackle.

Diagram #4. Shuffle Step

The center and the guard have the same technique on a 3-technique defender. To avoid the gray area, the center shuffles to make up the space. When you have to make up space, shuffle laterally. If the backside tackle has to cut off a 3-technique defender on the offensive guard, he cannot prevent the penetration if he lead steps into the B gap. He has to shuffle laterally to give himself a better angle to cut off the defender. The coaching point on the shuffle steps is to keep the steps small and quick. Do not overextend the steps.

The next thing I want to talk about is the *lazy forearm* block. I have done this for years. The lazy forearm is the same principle as the double-under lift. When the blocker delivers the forearm, the surface he hits with is from the wrist to the elbow and up to the shoulder. He wants to hit with the back of the wrist and lift with his forearm. The blocker strains up with his forearm and tries to get the defender away from him. All the blocks performed in blocking should be strained blocks. We do not want to lean on the defender; we want to strain and get him away from us. When you lean into the defender, there is no "oomph" in the block.

The thing I do not like about the combination double-team is the use of the hands in the block. I do not believe the drive blocker can control the defender with his hands until the post blocker takes over the block. I feel more comfortable with the lazy forearm than the hand shiver.

In the combination block, there are a number of surfaces that can be used to fit the situation. If the blocker is taking the defender straight back, the lazy forearm is a good technique to use. However, if the linebacker is in a position to flow away from the drive blocker, we need another technique. The drive blocker may use an uppercut under the arm of the defender, which we call a *shoulder pry*, instead of the lazy forearm. However, in both cases, the blocker has a high leg on the defender with the off leg back in the direction he has to come off to block the linebacker. If he is comfortable with the hand check, he can use that on the defender, but his high leg is always to the defender with his back leg in a position to come off on the linebacker.

The blocking surfaces the blocker can use are a double-hand lockout, double-under climb, lazy forearm, uppercut, or hand check. The technique you use depends on the angle you need to block the defender.

A problem area for the offensive blocker occurs when he has to help another offensive blocker get on his block but has an assignment on a linebacker. If the offensive guard has a 1-technique defender in the A gap, that defender belongs to the center. His block is the linebacker. He wants to help the center but he has to block the linebacker. If he steps down on the defender, he cannot get into position to block the linebacker.

To help the center, he has to take the perfect angle to get to that linebacker. When you run inside-zone type plays, the offensive linemen can slow down. The guard takes a brace step with his outside foot. That aligns his shoulders in the proper angle to get to the linebacker. From that position, he steps back and hand shivers the 1-technique defender. He is still on the line of scrimmage and catapults off the defender toward the linebacker.

If the guard has to get wider in his assignment, we have another technique he can use (Diagram #5). He has to help the center with the 1 technique but is worried about the 5-technique defender spiking to the inside. If he takes the brace step as he did with the linebacker, it is possible for the spiking defender to get penetration. If he uses the brace step, he does not gain much ground to the outside. He can still see the slant coming and could possibly fall into a block, but the situation is not good. However, if he shuffles to the outside after the hand shiver to the 1 technique, he is on the line of scrimmage and has closed the distance to the outside. He has helped the center and still can become involved with the zone combination with the tackle to his outside.

Diagram #5. Shiver and Shuffle

The guard can use both the technique for the linebacker block and the slanting tackle. The technique involves active footwork. The guard takes his brace step with his outside foot and steps with the inside foot back toward the 1 technique to deliver the hand shiver. The guard does not look at the 1-technique defender; he watches the 5-technique defender. If the 5-technique defender is working to the outside, the guard works up to the next level to the linebacker. We talked earlier about that technique. If the 5 technique is spiking to the

inside, he shuffles to the outside to close the distance. If the guard does not shuffle, the 5 technique is in the gray area and splits the blockers.

That gives the offensive blocker two ways he can help the center and still perform his assignment in the zone scheme. There has to be some communication between the guard and tackle so that the tackle knows what the guard is going to do. If the guard tells the tackle to *tag*, that means he is coming outside in the zone combination. The tackle knows the guard is working the combination block with him and can let the defender go if he spikes.

Let me talk about some weird stuff that coaches ask me about. This point comes up quite a bit. In this defensive alignment, there is a 3 technique on the outside shoulder of the guard and a 7 technique on the inside shoulder of the tight end (Diagram #6). The strong safety is down to the outside, and the Sam linebacker aligns in the A gap. There is a 1-technique defender to the backside and a Mike linebacker in the backside B gap. If your blocking scheme makes the guard, tackle, and tight end responsible for the Sam linebacker, 3 technique, and 7-technique defender, that, in my opinion, is a bad blocking scheme.

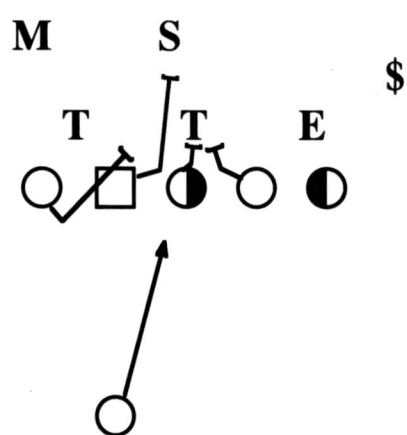

Diagram #6. Block Combinations

The better scheme is to put the center on the Sam linebacker and make him the designated blocker. That pushes the guard, tackle, and tight end to the frontside. Those rules are better than the guard and tackle trying to block the 3 technique and letting the Sam linebacker run through the A gap.

If you have the exact landmarks for the inside zone, the techniques of the guard and tackle are defined. The center takes the Sam linebacker, and the guard and tackle double-team the 3 technique on the inside zone play.

If we run the ball outside the guard, we still bring the center to the A gap to stop the run-through of the Sam linebacker. The guard and tackle work the combination on the 3-technique defender. The difference is the guard does not worry about the Sam linebacker running through to the inside. He can place his helmet into the 3 technique and go after him more aggressively. The tackle can hand check the 3 technique and get to the Sam linebacker. When we do this, we want to run the ball wide enough that we do not have to worry so much about the backside.

I want to talk about that technique a little more (Diagram #7). If we have a 3 technique and a 9 technique with the Sam linebacker over the tackle, we have to use some of the footwork we talked about earlier. The guard puts his head to the outside of the 3 technique. The tackle does not come down on the 3 technique. He runs what we call an up, which is a tackle-bubble technique. He takes his brace step to the outside and steps with his second step to the 3 technique. That gives him body presence on the defender.

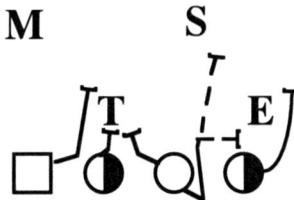

Diagram #7. Up

He does not avoid the 3 technique in an effort to block the linebacker. He hand shivers the 3 technique but can see the 9 technique. If, for some reason, the 9-technique defender spikes to the inside, the tackle uses his shuffle steps and blocks the spike. He is not very strong in that position, but he can get the job done.

I want to show you something that there is no answer for. I am thinking off the top of my head, but I want to show you this. If the defense plays a 37 alignment to the tight end with the Sam linebacker over the tackle, your play selection needs to consider those factors. If you run a play over the guard, the Sam linebacker falls right back into the hole. The guard turns out on the 3 technique and the tackle cannot keep the Sam linebacker out of the A gap.

To block the Sam linebacker, you have to run something to the outside. That presents another problem. To run the stretch play, the tackle and tight end combination block for the 7 technique and the Sam linebacker. The problem is the 3 technique. If the guard cannot overpower the defender, he makes the ball cut back right into the Sam linebacker. People that know how to play the zone play align the Sam linebacker deep, and he makes all the tackles. The 3 technique will make the ball bend to the inside, and the Sam linebacker comes back and makes the tackle. If you can get the Sam linebacker to flow to the outside, you are golden. However, teams that know how to play the zone do not flow the Sam linebacker. They play him deep and he stays home.

When you run the ball to the 3 and 7 techniques, there are better ways to attack it. The percentages of making yardage are better if you use a blocking scheme that releases the tight end and sends a back to block the Sam linebacker. Or, run right at him and let the tackle come off on him. You can also run the ball real wide with a G scheme, a down block, or a wide zone. That is why the defense plays the 3 technique, 7 technique, and Sam linebacker in those positions. The point I am making is that there are problems running to the 3 technique, and the wider you run, the more you make the defenders move. If two blockers have to block two defenders and one of the defenders is inside of them, you may as well block it like a double-team. I hope I did not lose anybody on that stuff.

I have been to a lot of colleges that run the shotgun offense. I have figured out the play because I have been to about 15 of them and watched their film. The mistake that colleges make occurs with the running back. The runner runs too wide in their zone schemes. If they run the jet sweep, that is fine. When they run the zone read, the running back should be running up the butt of the center.

What happens is the blockers are blocking zone to the outside. The ball starts to get wide and then cuts back. When the ball cuts back, all the defenders fall off the blockers back inside. The running back is not hitting the hole. He cannot get to the hole because he is so far offset. The best plays I am seeing are the jet sweep or the up-the-middle run.

I want to talk about the run to the split end side. To the split end side, most of the time the defense aligns with a 5 technique and a 1 technique with the linebacker in the B gap. The corner aligns on the wide receiver with the safety over the top. The one-back zone to the split end side used to be one of the best plays in football because there is no one outside.

The play we run in pro football to the split end side is the Bob play (Diagram #8). On the play, the guard blocks down on the 1-technique defender. The tackle turns out on the 5-technique defender, and the fullback isolates the linebacker. I want to talk about the tackle's block on the defensive end. When I coached at Buffalo, I turned my tackles out on Jason Taylor and he was beating the crap out of us. He was two gapping and running over the offensive tackles. The head coach, Mike Mularkey, was furious because we could not block him.

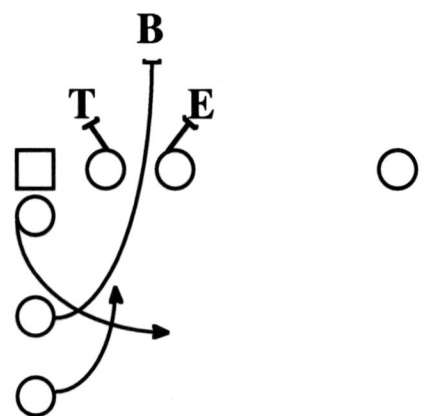

Diagram #8. Bob

I told him that on the Bob play, we should keep the tackle in a two-point stance and pass block him. The tackle took a kick-slide step toward the defensive end, gathered himself, and pass blocked him. When we tried to turn out on him in the regular blocking scheme, the end squashed the tackle, his butt was in the hole, and the running back could not see. When we used the pass drop scheme, we got separation, width, and depth, and the play worked better. Because the slide steps were short, if the defensive end went inside, he could adjust his blocking. If the defensive end thought it was pass, he had the tendency to rush upfield instead of straight into the blocker where he could two-gap him.

The next thing I learned from a guy by the name of Jeff Backus at Detroit. The tackle is on an island when he plays to the split end side. He has a problem picking up the defensive end on a pinch stunt to the inside. He taught me to get the offensive tackle to chop his feet as quickly as he could. If the tackle tried to two-step him, the defensive end beats him to the inside. They are too quick, even if you do get the second foot on the ground. You are always kind of edging the defensive end. You never get in front of him. By chopping the feet, you have a chance.

If the ball is coming inside the tackle and the defensive end pinches into the gap, the back does not have time to bounce the ball to the outside. The tackle has to set, turn out, or chop his feet and block the defensive end.

If we run the tight inside zone play to the split end side, the tackle can turn out on the defensive end because it does not matter whether his butt is in the hole. However, if the play comes inside the tackle, he has to get some separation to make the hole bigger. If the tackle has quick feet, he can get his head inside and get his inside arm under the defensive end's shoulder.

When you run the ball to the openside, you need to run either into the gap, inside the guard, or wide. If you run the play at the butt of the tackle, it puts too much pressure on the tackle's block. If the running back runs at the butt of the offensive tackle, either the running back or the tackle knows what to do. The running back is on top of the offensive tackle immediately and cannot make a decision about where to run the ball. When the ball is run inside the tackle or outside the tackle, there is space and the running back can tell what to do with the ball.

In the zone-blocking scheme, you have to find some way to get two offensive blockers shoulder to shoulder as they are coming off the ball. If the center and guard are going to work on a 3-technique defender in combination, you have to get them shoulder to shoulder to protect them from getting into the gray area. Instead of the center lead stepping into the A gap and up to the middle linebacker, he wants to get to his guard and get shoulder to shoulder. After that occurs, they both work up the field.

What is happening in the zone scheme is the 3 technique is not responding to the zone step of the guard. He lets the guard zone step to the outside and he plays off the inside shoulder of the guard. That means the guard has overreached and the 3 technique has split the offensive combination block. To prevent that from happening, the guard puts his helmet slightly outside the midline, and the center comes off shoulder to shoulder with the guard. Leave no space between the guard and center— that controls the down defender.

The center reads the middle linebacker as he gets shoulder to shoulder with the guard. If the linebacker is at normal depth, the center gets two hands on the 3 technique and pushes him outside. If the down linemen shades the center in the gap, the center puts his helmet underneath him and blocks him. If the linebacker is tight to the line of scrimmage, the center puts one hand on the 3 technique and keeps his eyes on the linebacker. He never looks at the down lineman. He feels him with his hands. He watches the linebacker. The point I am making is that in the zone play, get the combination blockers next to each other and do not leave any space between them. That is easy to say and hard to do.

This next point is something I have been saying for a long time: If there is a man in the gap, there is no gap. I let the guards and tight ends change their split. I have been doing this for a long time. Dick LaBeau says he knows when he is playing McNally because he sees no splits. When my linemen come to the line of scrimmage, they adjust their splits to close the gaps. If the guard has a 3 technique aligned on his outside shoulder, he moves his split to be foot to foot with the offensive tackle.

The defense knows that when we do that, we will run a power, double-team, or a backside zone block. The defense could take a noseguard and drop him into the gap between the center and guard. However, they will not take the 3 technique and move him into the gap because they have a defensive scheme they have to play. If you have two offensive linemen that work together, put them foot to foot.

The other lineman that I let adjust his split is the tight end. If there is a 5 technique aligned on the tackle and the tight end has a double-team with the tackle, the tight end moves foot to foot with the tackle. Another time you can split the tight end is when the Sam linebacker has backer force on a running play. How do you know the Sam linebacker has the run support? You know because the strong safety is in the half field. Move the tight end out to two to three yards. That widens the hole to the inside. If the center has a shade nose in the gap, the guard to that side gets foot to foot with the center. That tells the defense you are going to run isolation to the frontside or zone away from the shade. Why would you zone block with that big of a split? Close the gap and the zone scheme is easier.

Let me talk about something that may not come up but it is interesting to see it when it works. The situation is a combination block for the backside linebacker. The center and right guard have a 1 technique in the playside gap. They are responsible for the nose and Mike linebacker. The problem is the Mike linebacker running through the backside A gap. If the play is wide enough, it is not a problem. However, if the play is tighter, it presents a problem.

I do not see too many people doing this type of scheme. I used to talk about it and people thought I was crazy (Diagram #9). The nose in the 1-technique alignment is responsible for the A gap. If the center can shove him to the B gap, there is a hole. The Mike linebacker has the backside A gap. The call we gave was, "Stick." It was a word that meant nothing. It could have been anything. The center moved sideways with a high right leg and shoved the nose into the B gap. His back leg was back. After he shoved the nose, we worked upfield with his back leg back to intercept the Mike linebacker.

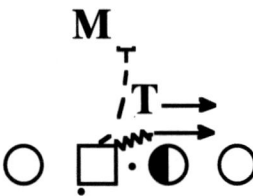

Diagram #9. Stick

If the guard came down on the nose without the center's help, that was an uncomfortable block for him. The center shoved the nose over to the block of the guard and released back for the linebacker. If he blocked the nose, he opened the backside A gap and the Mike linebacker ran through the gap.

The same situation exists with the backside 3 technique (Diagram #10). The tackle steps sideways and shoves the 3 technique inside and steps back for the 7 technique or the linebacker coming into the backside gap. When he shoves the 3 technique to the inside, he creates a hole to his inside. Remember what I said about the gaps. If there is a man in the gap, there is no gap. The backside guard moves out toward the tackle, and the frontside guard moves in toward the center.

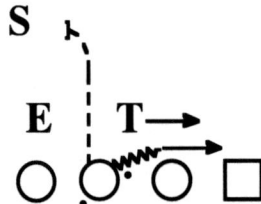

Diagram #10. Backside Stick

The next thing I am going to tell you will convince you that I am crazy. The defense reads the stances of the offensive linemen. I want to screw with the defense and mess up their minds with the stance we get in. If I put the right tackle in a left-handed stance, everyone assumes he is going to his right. That is when I use the reverse or naked bootleg. The reason you want to do that is to disguise the technique you want to use. So many times in your blocking technique, you need a high leg.

If the right guard has a play coming to his inside, he wants his outside leg to be high in the block. He wants to blunt the force of the 3 technique to his outside. If he is in the right-handed stance, his footwork will be backward to get the outside leg high. He aligns in the left-handed stance and steps with the outside foot to the 3-technique defender. That puts his outside leg as the high leg. Everyone assumes, since he is in the left-handed stance, he is going to the left.

If the left guard has an inside shade he has to cut off, he gets in a right-handed stance and makes the block. The next time we run the bootleg to that side, the left guard gets in the right-handed stance and the defense goes the wrong way. Go ahead and mess with the defense! The offensive coaches get so nervous about that they cannot breathe. The defense is so stupid, who cares what you show them? Get in the stance you need to get the job done, and the defense will be so confused they will not know what to do. In high school, if your players are having trouble getting things done, change their stances to make the movement easier. If they have to go left, put them in the left-handed stance. If they are going right, put them in the right-handed stance.

Everyone talks about four hands and four eyes in double-team blocking (Diagram #11). If the offense runs the tight zone in the A gap, there will be a double-team between the center and guard, if there is a 1 technique in that gap. The center and guard have to double the nose and watch the Mike linebacker. The center and guard have to get a square double-team on the nose. The center cannot come off at an angle and double. The center and guard are hip to hip and foot to foot in their drive.

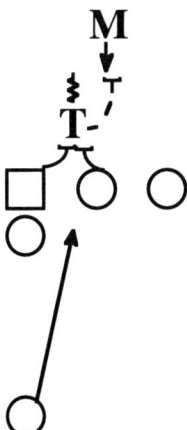

Diagram #11. Square Double-Team

The guard and center get two hands on the nose, but both of them are watching the Mike linebacker. If the center buries his helmet into the nose, he cannot see the linebacker. Whether you perfect the techniques, there are times you have to stay square because of where the running back goes. If the running back goes wider, the center can get his head across the nose. The bottom line is to make sure you know when the double has to stay square because of where the ball is going.

The down block is a critical block. I cannot count the number of hours we have spent on the down block. I coached 45 years, and I cannot come up with any sound rules for the down block. Do you put your head in front or behind? Do you put the helmet in the armpit? The best way to down block is to throw the head across the defender and leg whip him. However, that is illegal. The simplest way to down block is to pass block. If the tackle blocks down on a 3-technique defender, he takes a power step with his inside foot. He follows that with a double underarm punch. That stops the penetration, and if he tries to get outside, we stay on him as a pass block.

We developed this because of the nose tackle in Minnesota. We pulled our center and blocked down with the guard. When the guard came down on the angle, there was space between the down block and the center's pull. The nose tackle would grab the center so he could not get out. When we used the power step and shuffle down on the pass block technique, there was no space for the nose tackle

to grab the center. You do not need to blow the defender out. You need to cut him off and keep him from pursuing.

We teach a regular double-team. For you coaches that use the hands, you are not necessarily wrong. The post man on the right side is better in a left-handed stance. The reason is the right foot does not have as far to go to get into the block. We step with the left foot and make contact on the right foot. That puts the high leg to the side of the double-team. We bring the right forearm up into the defender and run with the left arm pumping. He uses the forearm because he has to worry about the run-through of the linebacker.

The drive blocker or man coming down on the double-team has to take two steps to get the punch I talked about in the beginning. I do not want the drive man to step with his inside foot and make contact. I want him to step with his outside foot and explode with his inside foot into the block. That puts his inside leg up as the high leg. I want the drive blocker to come down with a double under and get his hands on the defender. That gives control to the double-team. The post blocker has his forearm on the defender and the drive blocker has his hands into the defenders hip, lifting him.

If the linebacker is flowing over the top, you can take the double-team north and south. However, if the linebacker runs under the double-team, the post man has to get off for the block. We use an inside rip to escape from the double-team. When the post man rips through to get off the block, the defender moves inside with the post blocker trying to control him. The drive blocker uses the down-block technique I just showed you to complete the double-team.

This next situation is interesting, and I had a lot of trouble understanding how to make this block. The situation is a backside combination block on a tight zone play (Diagram #12). The backside guard and tackle had to block a 3-technique tackle and a 20-technique linebacker so the zone play could break backside. I could never understand how to perform that block. The tackle seemed to always knock the 3 technique into the hole.

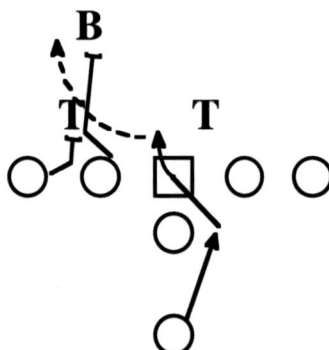

Diagram #12. Backside Zone Block

I knew what to do with the guard. He stepped to the 3 technique and hit him with his inside foot back. If the linebacker ran through the gap, he came off on the linebacker. The backside tackle had to align off the ball and shuffle down to get under the 3 technique. He had to get under him before he could drive him. It was like a square double-team. He could not push on the defender until he had inside leverage.

I listened to Howard Mudd talk about the reach block years ago. If I am a backside tackle trying to cut off a 3 technique, there is a coaching point. You need to get off the ball in your stance. When he steps, he wants to step back and land on the toe of the inside foot. That allows him to get space and get by the defender. If the tackle comes flat to the line, he has no chance to make a block. You can shuffle and drive, but you have to get him hooked. To hook the defender, you have to get depth off the ball and land on the toe. By doing that, the blocker may be able to run laterally. That means pulling down the line of scrimmage with the shoulder square to the line of scrimmage.

The deeper you step off the line of scrimmage, the more space the blocker has to go to the outside. The fastest way to cut off or reach a defender is to use the crossover step. If the blocker is going to cross over, he pivots on his right heel. When you pivot on the heel, the crossover step is easy and quick. If you pick up the lead foot or open with it, the back foot does not move. However, when you pivot on the heel, you do not waste a step and you cover so much more ground. The fastest way to move with zero power is to pivot on the heel and cross

over with the foot. That is the fastest way to get to the linebacker on the backside.

When we play teams that use the pirate schemes on defense, we handle that with wide zone plays (Diagram #13). The pirate stunt spikes the 3 technique and 7 technique into the A gap and B bap. We take foot-to-foot splits and fire out on a slight angle. If you do, the defender will come right to the blockers. If they do not come to the offensive blocker, we run the wide zone play.

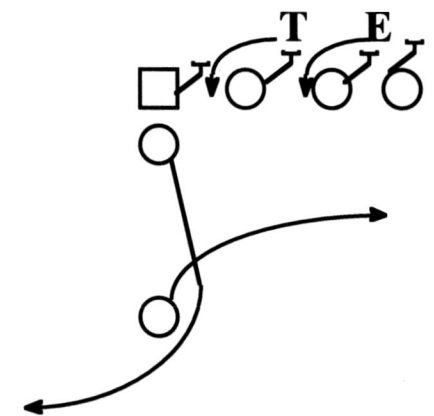

Diagram #13. Pirate

The pirate is a good reason not to run too many zone plays to the 3 technique. If you want to run to the 3 technique, you have to get outside more often. If you run too many zone plays to the 3 technique, you will have problems.

With that said, let me show you what I love running to the 3 technique (Diagram #14). I like to run it from a 3x1 set. In my blocking schemes, I do not want to block a defender that is behind me. I do not want to step to the right when my assignment is to my left. I want to run a tight inside zone play at the inside leg of the guard. The center's assignment is the Mike linebacker. The back runs to the inside leg of the guard and reads the 3 technique. It is easier to read the 3 technique when you run at the inside leg of the guard.

The backside guard has a tough block. However, since the ball is running tight toward the guard, the shuffle and drive block by the backside guard will work. The backside tackle shuffles and moves up on the Will linebacker. The backside end is unblocked.

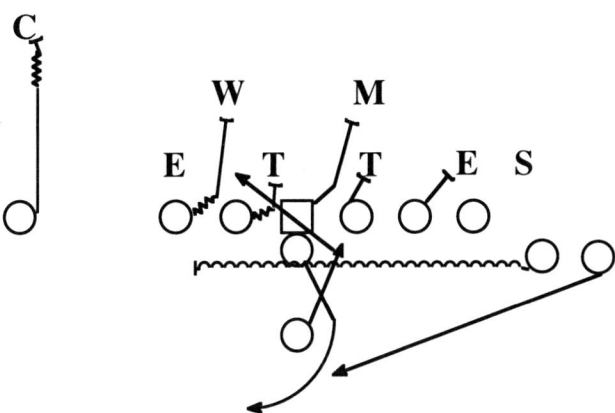

Diagram #14. Tight Zone

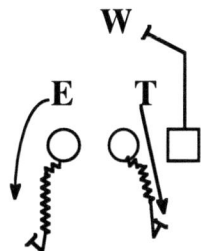

Diagram #15. Draw Blocking

We always run a reverse fake by the wide receiver, or we can bring a receiver in motion and block the backside defensive end.

The center does not run up to the Mike linebacker. He has from A gap to A gap as his blocking area. He moves toward the 3-technique defender. If the 3 technique spikes into the A gap, the center blunts his charge and has his backside foot back. That allows him to block the Mike linebacker if he falls back into the A gap.

The companion play is the one-back zone play to the openside of the formation. If there are too many defenders to the openside of the formation, I run the wide stretch play.

The wide zone play to the 3-technique side is the companion to the one-back zone to the openside of the formation. Everyone to the wideside is stretching to the outside. The tackle stops the 3 technique, and the ball breaks back off-tackle. The defense is going to blitz, and someone is going to loop to the outside. If you stop the defender looping to the outside, there is a big hole.

When you run a draw play, try not to double-team anyone—let them penetrate (Diagram #15). If you have a 1 technique and a Will linebacker to the backside, do not block the center on the 1-technique defender. Let the guard block him, and let him penetrate. Sneak the center up the field and block him on the Will linebacker. You will have a better play if you do not block it like a run. Let the defense penetrate.

PASS PROTECTION

In pass protection, I have three angles I teach. I teach the kick-slide at a 45-degree angle. That is *angle A* to me. *Angle A+* is more of a vertical set. I hate this angle, but we have to use it because of the speed of the defensive ends. The vertical set is a deeper set but never straight back. It is back at an angle always trying to widen the pocket. The third, and my most favorite set, is a *jump set*. The tackle never jumps the defensive end from the get-go. He kicks and slides to the outside and replants the brace foot. Once he plants the brace foot, he blocks the defensive end as he did on the turnout block on the Bob play. He kicks out, slides, replants the brace foot, and duck steps to the defender with rapid short steps. I would use this set on every play except the T-E. I would use it on that play if the guard did a good enough job of shoving the 3-technique defender.

The big problem in pass blocking is no one knows how to pivot. In the pass block, the blocker has to turn to push the rusher past the quarterback. That is the point where the rusher starts to bend in to the quarterback. That point is generally on the third step of the blocker. When the blocker turns to push on the rusher, his inside foot hangs and he cannot get a good push. The reason his inside foot hangs is because the blocker never pivots off the inside foot. He kick-slides to the outside and the inside foot is flat on the ground.

When he kicks out and slides, he has to get on his inside toe and not his foot. When he reaches the point at which he has to turn and push the defender, he can get a full pivot with his body. That means instead of facing the sideline, he faces the opposite goal line. In that position, he can push the rusher past the quarterback with no problem. By being on the inside toe, the inside foot pivots all the way and allows the blocker to get a better angle to push the defender.

On the kick-slide to the outside, the blocker can move faster if he is on the outside toe. If the defender is tight to the blocker, he can kick-slide and keep his outside foot on the ground. However, if the defender is wide and the blocker has to get out there in a hurry, he needs to get on his outside toe. That is the fastest way to move. In the tight rush, the blocker is on his feet. On the wide rush, he is on his toes.

When the rusher comes upfield, if the blocker turns outside, the rusher blows the blocker back into the quarterback. The only way I know to keep the blocker square is to take the outside foot and pigeon-toe it. Do not let the blocker turn and look at the rusher. If they do, they will open up the hips and the rusher will come over the top of them. They can look at the rusher, but they must keep their shoulders square. As the blocker kicks out at an angle, he jabs out with his outside hand. The pigeon-toed stance and the jabbing motion with the outside hand keeps the blocker square to the line of scrimmage.

On his third step, the rusher will generally do something. He will continue to run upfield, come into the blocker, or try a move of some kind. If the rusher does not attack the blocker on the third step, the blocker continues to get depth. If the rusher bends and tries to come to the quarterback, the blocker pivots and pushes him by the quarterback. If the rusher tries to make a move, the blocker punches him with the hand he has been jabbing and resets his hands.

If the blocker has a loose 3- or 5-technique alignment on him, his target is the inside armpit of the rusher. The inside target keeps the blocker from overextending and losing his center of gravity. If he has help on the block, the target is the outside number. The blocker uses a kick-slide to get to the outside. As the defender approaches the blocker,

the blocker punches him with his inside hand on the inside shoulder of the rusher. The blocker wants to get in front of the rusher using his feet.

When the blocker punches the point of the shoulder with his inside hand, it keeps him balanced. If the defender reaches out and grabs the blocker, the blocker brings his hand and arm underneath the defender's arm and resets the hand on the defender. The outside hand does not get involved with the blocker unless the blocker wants to punch into the chest of the defender with the outside hand. We do not need the outside hand in this technique.

If the rusher is close to the offensive lineman, the target is the same as the loose rusher. However, we do not punch to the target, the blocker uses a double or single under lift on the rusher. If the rusher has long arms and punches into the blocker's chest, the blocker uses a double under and locks the rusher's elbows. The blocker cannot reach the chest of the defender, but he does not need to. He uses the double under as an elbow lift, and he does not lunge at the defender.

If the rusher is working the blocker on the T-E stunt, the blocker uses the same footwork as he does on run blocking. If the blocker is working the rusher outside, the blocker wants to throw him as he did in his run blocking. When he gets to the position to throw the rusher, he wants his inside foot back. He throws with his inside arm and foot. That is why you do not need the outside hand involved with this technique. If the blocker puts the outside hand on the rusher, he may as well run block him.

If the defender is loose in his alignment, the blocker uses his kick-slide and punches the shoulder point with the inside hand. If the defender is tight on the blocker, he does his two-step movement but he does not gain ground to the outside. His hand movement is a single or double under into the defender. If the defender is head-up the blocker, the blocker does his two-step footwork in place and uses the double under. If the defender is slightly inside the blocker, the blocker wants to move as far inside as he can with his footwork and use the double-under hand movement. If the defender is far inside of the blocker, the blocker gets as far to the inside as he can. He uses a single under and an outside shoulder punch. He uses the outside shoulder punch in case the defender tries to redirect outside.

If the defender is close to the blocker, he uses a double-under hand movement. If he is farther away, the blocker uses a single under and a shoulder punch. If the defender tries to move inside on the blocker, the blocker grabs the belt of the defender and pulls him inside into the defender.

Fellas, we are done. Thank you for coming, and I hope to see you again.

ABOUT THE AUTHOR

Throughout Coach McNally's career, Jim was one of the most highly regarded position coaches in the league. Coach McNally made an immediate impact on every team when hired to coach their offensive line.

With the Bills in 2005, McNally helped second-year tackle Jason Peters develop into a starter. Peters, an undrafted free agent and former tight end at Arkansas, started the final nine games of the season at right tackle. The line paved the way for Willis McGahee's career-high 1,247 yards. With the Bills in 2004, McNally tutored an offensive line that limited opponents to 38 sacks, the lowest number allowed by a Bills team since 1998. Also with the Bills, McNally's line paved the way for Willis McGahee to rush for 1,128 yards and 13 touchdowns in 11 starts.

Prior to retiring from the NFL with the Bills, McNally coached the offensive line for the New York Gi-ants (1999 to 2003) and helped maintain offensive line success with little personnel continuity on the line during his tenure. In 2000, McNally guided an offensive line with three new players to a successful season, which culminated in the Giants' rise to the NFC Championship.

Prior to joining the Giants, McNally coached the offensive line for the Carolina Panthers (1995 to 1998) and the Cincinnati Bengals (1980 to 1994). In

McNally's time at Carolina, the Panthers advanced to the NFC Championship game in only the team's second season of existence.

Jim's longest tenure was as the offensive line coach for the Cincinnati Bengals. In his time at Cincinnati, McNally helped establish one of the most potent rushing attacks in the league from 1986 to 1990. He coached Hall of Fame offensive tackle Anthony Muñoz and the Bengals advanced to the Super Bowl two times during his tenure.

Before entering the NFL coaching ranks, McNally coached the offensive line at Wake Forest University (1978 to 1979), Boston College (1975 to 1977), and Marshall University (1971 to 1974). McNally initiated his coaching career at his alma mater, University at Buffalo, and coached there for six seasons (1965 to 1970).

Originally from Buffalo, McNally played guard at the University at Buffalo from 1961 to 1964 and the combination of his playing career and his coaching expertise earned him a spot in the university's Hall of Fame. Now retired from coaching, Jim is nationally known for his clinics on offensive line coaching, which he conducts in the off-season.

MCNALLY AT A GLANCE

- 2004-2005: Buffalo Bills, Offensive Line Coach
- 1999-2003: New York Giants, Offensive Line Coach
- 1995-1998: Carolina Panthers, Offensive Line Coach
- 1980-1994: Cincinnati Bengals, Offensive Line Coach
- 1978-1979: Wake Forest University, Offensive Line Coach
- 1975-1977: Boston College, Offensive Line Coach
- 1971-1974: Marshall University, Offensive Line Coach
- 1965-1970: University of Buffalo, Offensive Line Coach

SHORT-YARDAGE/GOAL-LINE/FOUR-MINUTE OFFENSE

Kansas City Chiefs

It is good to be here. As Bob pointed out, I have a long resume. I started coaching when I was 12 years old. That is how I made all those stops. It has been a nice ride. Someone once told me, "If you enjoy what you are doing, you never work a day in your life." I have been in the National Football League for 32 years and have been in organized football for 56 years. I have spent most of my life in football. I can tell you it is what keeps me going.

I enjoy coming to these events. Looking out at the audience, I see coaches at different stages of their careers. I can only tell you how it feels from my perspective. I do not want to be overphilosophical, but when it is all said and done and you look back, it is all about the players. This business is all about winning and competition, and the competiveness is what keeps us in the game. However, you can never underestimate the influence that you have on the men you coach.

I think that might be the most significant thing about what I have done with my career. I do not want to talk about my career in the past tense, but I actually thought about retiring this past year. In fact, I retired for 10 days. I could not stand it and went back to coaching.

One of the pleasures I get is wearing my Super Bowl ring. Occasionally, I go back and look at pictures of teams that I have been on and teams I have coached. However, the things I enjoy most are the calls and letters that I get from former players.

I had a call the other day from a player I coached in 1975 at Southern Methodist University. We were playing in Dallas, and he wanted to know if we could get together. Those types of things are what inspire me and keep me going. Too many times, we get caught up in the day-to-day world that we live in. It is

very competitive, and there is a lot of anxiety in what we do. However, we continue to do it. I want you to stop and think about the human element in what you are doing. You do not know how much you touch them and how it will affect them down the road.

I am a football coach because of my high school football coach. My high school football coaches made such an impression on me that I never wanted to be anything but a coach. When I went to college, there was no doubt in my mind that I was going to be a football coach and go back to Western Pennsylvania and coach high school football. I told my Dad that one day I might be a head coach or even an athletic director. That was my goal when I came out of college.

I have been lucky and I was at the right place at the right time. I have done a little more with the game than I ever thought I would do. I am from Pittsburgh, and my father worked in the steel mills there for 40 years. He was an immigrant who came to this country from Scotland. I had been coaching for about eight years in a small college when I got married. I went home to visit my father. My father was a very stoic man and there were not a lot of hugs and kisses in my family. It was a great family to grow up in, but my dad was not one for showing affection. He took me aside and told me that I had a wife and a family on the way and it was time for me to give all this football crap up and get a real job. That was my father's perspective, but I am glad I did not listen to him.

You are a role model. One of the reasons I am who I am today is because I was impressed at a young age by a football coach. Another reason I am able to do what I do is that many people along the way have shared their knowledge with me. That is why I like to come to these events. I will talk to any coach at any time, and I will speak at clinics like this. I think sharing is a responsibility I have. When I started coaching, I did not know anything about it. Someone taught me how to coach. Somebody taught me how to scout, organize a practice, and break down tape. I would not have known how to do those things if somebody had not taken the time to teach me.

I feel a responsibility, and what I am trying to say to you is share what you know. I have been in places where I felt I was working in the CIA, where you could not tell anybody anything. I will tell you anything you want to know. At the end of the day, we all know it is about preparation. It is about how you package what you are selling and how you teach it.

The game of football is like Darwinism—it is always changing. I am trying to relate some of the things to you that have helped me in my career. You have to keep an open mind. I know we all have a philosophy and a certain way of doing things that have been successful or you would not continue doing them. However, change in the game of football is inevitable. Football continues to evolve because of coaches like you. You are creative people, but we are the biggest copycats in the world. Everything you do has been done before. You may put your fingerprint on it, but it is not new.

The one thing I keep saying to myself is what my mother told me. She said the trouble with knowing everything is you cannot learn anything new. That is the message I want to pass on to you. I am undergoing a new experience. It is becoming hard to evaluate college talent for the draft. We watch a lot of tape and visit a lot of schools. The problem is the college game, at many levels, is changing.

You can watch a lineman at some school in the spread offense and for 13 games, they are in a two-point stance. There is one player in the draft that will probably make 50 million dollars. I watched him in 13 games and never saw him in a three-point stance. The head coach wants to draft him but he wants to know if he can run block. All I can tell him is he can cut off and turn people. I know he can pass protect for .9 seconds because the ball comes out that quick. I know he can run outside on a speed or wide receiver screen. That is all I know after watching him for 12 weeks.

My point to you is to keep an open mind and that change is inevitable. You have to make sure when you change, you are changing for good reasons. Do not be one of those coaches that are so stubborn that you refuse to do anything new. You have to be able to adapt. To survive, you must have adaptability. I read a lot about other coaches in other sports. I read about successful organizations and successful people. I like to know what they are thinking. I remember reading a book about Lou Holtz and one thing stuck with me. In this book, Lou Holtz was talking about the word *win*. He broke it down into terms of your daily activities or off-season program or whatever you do. He said that *WIN* stood for *What's Important Now*.

That thought stuck with me. This has a bearing on what you are going to do for the season or what your off-season program is going to be like. You could be trying to organize your training camp or your playbook. Or it could be something as simple as organizing your practice schedule.

We have a program in the NFL called OTA. It is a practice organization for offensive linemen. It is a nightmare because you cannot wear pads. We had our first OTA the other day and I was sitting in my meeting room. They wanted me to put in seven running plays, five protections, and one screen the next day. They wanted me to do that in an hour-and-a-half meeting.

That is an overwhelming amount of material you have to present. I am a new coach working in a new system with a new staff. It is an illustration of *what's important now*. I have to sit down and think about what is the most important thing I have to accomplish tomorrow. For the last 10 years, that has been my motto. I practice *WIN* when I am in a situation and I have to decide what to do.

You have to prioritize your list and start working on it. If you do not get to the bottom of the list, you just do not get to it. However, you cover the most important things on the list. *"It is alright to evaluate the past and focus on the future. However, you have to know what you need to get done today."*

I have had an interesting couple of months because we have a new staff. Everyone comes in from different places with different ideas. I have always believed that all the good ideas you have and what you are doing does not matter. It is not whether the ideas are any good; it is the players that you are asking to do them. You have to modify what you want to do to what your players can do. You might leave many good ideas on the table, but at the end of the day, the players have to play.

I believe two things very strongly. The first thing is to go by what you see. If you turn on the tape, you are what you see on the tape. I just went through a frustrating football season, and it probably cost us our jobs. I had been with the Tampa Bay Buccaneers for seven years. This past year, we were 9-3 at the bye week. We never won another game, finished 9-7, and missed the playoffs. I heard everyone talk about "shoulda, coulda, woulda," but at the end of the day, you are what your record says.

We were a 9-7 football team. We won some we should not have won early and lost some that we should not have lost late. You are what you are on tape. If you think you have a hell of a player, put the tape on. If you do not see a hell of a player, you have misevaluated him. If you are ready to run a player off, put the tape on. If he is making plays, then have the guts to say, "This player is better than I thought."

I tell my players that. I just met my offensive line for the first time about a month ago. There were 15 players in the room, and there was a lot of anxiety in there. That is understandable because they know a new coaching staff means changes. I told them that everyone starts with a clean slate. I told them I had three things I was going to ask of them. When I watch tape, these are the things I ask myself. The first one is "Does the player know what to do?" The second question is "Is the player trying to do things the way you asked him to do

them?" Sometimes, when you get to pro ball, you compromise that thought.

Early in my career, I had the pleasure of working with John Hannah, the Hall of Fame offensive guard for the New England Patriots. I did not say *coach*, I said *work with*. After working with him, I thought I was a good coach. When I went to the next job, the things I thought I was doing well just were not working with other players. That showed me it was not the technique so much as it was the talent. John could do it any way. Unless you have superior talent, you want to look and see if your players are doing it the right way.

The third thing I look for is the conditioning of the linemen. I want to know if they are in shape. If they are not in shape, there will come a point in time where they do not care who they block or whether they are doing it right. All they are interested in doing is getting it done. That is not good enough.

I asked my players if they noticed I did not say anything about talent. Obviously, talent is the great equalizer. However, at the end of the day, if you do not know what you are trying to do and you are not going to try to do it the way I want it done, we cannot win with you. What we do may not be for everyone, but we know it works.

I ask my players when I have them in the meeting room if they know what "buyer beware" means. They think it has something to do with the lemon law. I tell them, "In this room, you better *buy* into what I am saying or *beware* of the consequences."

Football, to me, is like going to elementary school where you get the basics of reading, writing, and arithmetic. That is what is taught, and you learn it by repetition. Everything you know from that point on is based on how well you learned the fundamentals of reading, writing, and arithmetic. That is the way I coach the offense line. Every day we are going to do fundamentals.

I may be in the NFL, but I learned how to hit a Crowther sled in 1957 in high school. I still use the Crowther sled today. Somewhere along the line, someone showed me how to use chutes and boards. I use them today. I have a progression drill I do today that I did in college. I do it because it works. I do fundamentals every day. If they have pads on, we do them harder than if they are in shorts, but we do them every day.

In the off-season, you cannot hit anyone, but you can hit the sled and develop technique. The first day I meet the defensive line coach, I start to lobby for a drill between the offensive and defensive linemen. I call it the *pods drill*. I coached with Rod Marinelli, and that is what he called the drill. All you need is a ball, offensive linemen, defensive linemen, and no one else. We go 1-on-1, 2-on-1, and 3-on-1. We snap the ball and slam into each other. We emphasize two things. We emphasize *pad level* and *footwork*. The good thing about the drill is it is a low-risk injury drill. I have never had anyone hurt in this drill.

If we have an inside drill, I want to do this drill before that. I want to slam them into each other and get them lathered up. I do not want to get to 9-on-7 or an inside-run period and waste two or three plays while they get warmed up. I have only 12 plays in the drill and I do not want to waste any of them. The purpose of the drill is not to warm them up. The drill is about fit, pad level, and the first and second step. That is the only thing we work on during that drill.

I want to tell you a short story. In 2003, Tampa Bay played the Raiders in the Super Bowl in San Diego. We practiced in a beautiful stadium on Thursday. The other offensive coaches ran the offensive line off the stadium practice facility because they needed the field for a passing drill. We had to go behind the hedges that surrounded the field to practice. Rod Marinelli and I had one of those drills in kind of a little valley behind the hedges. The hitting was so loud and it echoed throughout the stadium, and they stopped practice on the other field. They thought we had broken out into an all-out brawl on the other side of the hedges.

The next thing we knew, all the support staff had left the main practice field and were peeking through the hedges to see what was going on. This drill is a great way to teach fundamentals; it is a great way to start a padded practice; and more than anything, it is a great way to develop attitude. Developing attitude is probably the most important of the three reasons to do this drill. Attitude is what it is all about. In this drill, the "low man wins." I use that expression all the time.

This type of play happens before I talk about any offense or even a play. You can take any player you have, regardless of his ability level, and make him better because of the fundamentals. If you take the fundamental approach to teaching, apply it on a daily basis, and stick with it, you will raise that player up to another level of play. It will be because of fundamentals and attitude.

In your meeting room, you have to talk your stuff. Then, you take them to the field and walk through it. However, when you blow the whistle, all the walking and talking is over. Then it becomes pad level, footwork, and attitude.

What I want to talk about today is grouping. In football, no matter what level you play on, it all boils down to situations. If you stop and think about the game, the situations arise in the game that define what we do. Many of us get caught up in the first- and second-down mentality. You spend most of your time practicing the plays that are the big picture for you. You need to break your preparation down and decide how much time you are going to allot for situations.

The majority of the game is a first-and-ten or a second-and-five or less. However, you are going to be in the red zone, be backed up, on the goal line, have short yardage, and four-minute situations. How many times have you started the game and been in great shape? The next thing you know, you are into the last four minutes of the game trying to hang on for the win. You need a plan for all those situations. The trick is not the plan, it is how much time you devote to practicing those plans.

Three weeks ago, we were talking about short yardage and goal-line offense. I have a passion for those situations. I got into all the things we did in those situations and was enthused talking about it. We put on the cut-ups and all that stuff must have been in my mind. We played 16 games and had only 22 plays of goal-line offense. I thought, we practiced all that time on the goal line and only had 22 plays in the entire season. We may have gone three weeks without being in that situation. You have to think about how much time you should devote to a goal-line situation. You have to spend time on it, and shame on you if you do not. There will come a time in the season where you will be in that situation two or three times.

You have to work on it, but how much time do you devote to it? How many short-yardage plays are there in a football game? When I say short yardage, I mean third or fourth-and-one. In a game, you may have only three short-yardage situations. I think short yardage is critical. However, I coach the players to play their butts off on every play because you never know which play will make the difference. I do know when you get to the goal line, you better put either six or three points on the scoreboard.

You have to do something special in those situations in terms of effort and execution. You affect the scoreboard in goal line, and you have a chance to keep your offense on the field in short yardage. Those situations are unusual situations. They require unusual execution. The biggest of those situations is the four-minute offense. You have to practice not going out of bounds and staying in the huddle. You must have a plan, but you must allocate enough time to practice it.

You have to give them a plan and allocate the time to practice it, but you cannot let it dominate the amount of time you practice. They should not demand more time because of the number of times during the season you use them. What I have gotten to is a small core of plays and an off-speed pitch that goes with each one of them. I use those plays in short-yardage, goal-line, and four-minute situations. That is our offense in those situations. If I can carry over those plays in the three situations, I have tripled my practice time for those situations.

No matter how hard you studied, you never knew what you were going to get in the short-yardage situations. If we played someone in the 12th week and watched 11 weeks of tape in those situations, we always got something different when we played them. When you select plays to run in that situation, you have to select plays that are adaptable.

The goal-line situation is something different. In our league, when it gets to a goal-line situation, everyone plays one of two defenses. Some teams play both of those defenses and jump in and out of them during the game. That also means you need plays that are adaptable to those defenses. That is the key statement I am trying to make right now. To be successful in those situations, you have to select certain plays that can adjust to those fronts. For every one of the situations, I have what I call a *commandment.*

SHORT-YARDAGE OFFENSE (TAMPA BAY BUCCANEERS)

- *Short yardage* is defined as third-and-one or fourth-and-inches. The quarterback will alert everyone in the huddle by saying, "Alert short yardage." You must prepare for a select group of plays.

- Understand that if we fail, we turn the ball over to the defense. Our goal is to convert *every* short-yardage situation.

- *Snap Count:* We will always go on one unless no snap or no play. We must hold the count at times. Alert stemming fronts, the quarterback will help us. We will use our otto and can packages. Don't always use can. Start to use scratch it.

- *Offensive Line:* Alignment is on the ball. Use four-point stances. Splits are one foot. Anticipate stunts and gap adjustments by the defense.

- You must anticipate a variety of fronts. Use what you practice and use your ability to adjust. Communication is a must.

- *All Blockers:* Hat placement and footwork are critical. Block low to high and finish. Do not allow penetration and get movement.

- *Running Backs:* No shifting unless called. Line up in final set and know what we need for the first down. We need great course discipline. Any shift by game plan will be rehearsed and completely understood.
- The plays we select as short yardage must be understood *completely* and must be blocked with maximum effort from everyone.
- Our can package will be featured in this situation. You must be adaptable versus opponents with multiple short-yardages defenses.
- *Play-Action:* This pass is our change-up to the run and has big-play potential. Our play-action protection must be detailed. We are great at faking. The quarterback must never take a sack in this situation, knowing we are going for it on fourth down.
- *Quarterbacks:* Always ask for a measurement prior to a huddle call. Know exactly what we need for the first down. (Inches? A full yard?)
- Keep your poise. It will be loud on the road. The tight end and wings must concentrate.
- Penalties and missed assignments will get you beat...period.

Every short-yardage meeting, I start out with a definition of short yardage. The snap count, in my opinion, must always be on *one* unless we have a no snap or no play, which I will cover in a minute. We use a nonrhythmic count, and the quarterback will alter his cadence to give the defense a chance to stem. That helps the offensive line because it allows them to see the defense after it moves.

In the short-yardage and goal-line situations, I want the offensive line to get as close to the ball as they can. That point is so important I have two coaches stand on either sideline to make sure we are as close to the ball as we can get. We know the defense will get as close to the ball as they can. They will stem their front, penetrate, and blitz you. However, they cannot get any closer than the tip of the ball, and we do not want to give them any room before we get on them. In the goal-line situation, penetration is an issue, and we have to block low to high to stop the penetration. We have to finish every block.

The play-action pass is part of the goal-line package, but we will not throw a play-action pass unless we plan to go for it on fourth down. If we have third-and-short, we want to run the ball. The running back has to know the distance he needs, and he has to lunge for that yard.

FOUR-MINUTE OFFENSE

- When there is less than four minutes left and we have the lead, we use the four-minute offense. It is key that we understand this situation *completely.*
- The enemy is the clock. Our goal is to make two first downs and finish the game on the field.
- Understand that the defense will do anything possible to get the ball back. Stingers are a must in this situation. Our communication and ball security must be top-notch.
- Do *not* go out of bounds. The last thing we want to do is stop the clock. Ballcarriers have to be careful on sideline plays.
- Penalties will stop the clock and put us way behind in the down-and-distance. They must be avoided.
- Running the football is a priority in this situation. Anticipate an A-gap run-through at all times.
- The quarterback must see the game clock and snap the ball with three seconds left.
- Absolutely no turnovers. We have a Pro-Bowl punter, and we will use him if necessary in this situation.

When we get into a four-minute period, everyone must understand the situation. We have to realize the enemy is the clock. No matter where we take the ball over, the goal is to get two first downs. In this situation, the offense should expect a variety of fronts. This is a different philosophy for the offensive line as opposed to the short-yardage situation. You do not want to tighten your line splits, but you want to be up on the ball.

The defense will take more risks in a four-minute situation than they will in short-yardage or goal-line situations. They are trying to get the ball back, and you are trying to kill the clock. In that situation, anything goes.

GOAL-LINE OFFENSE

- Goal-line offense begins at the four-yard line. The quarterback will alert everyone in the huddle by saying, "Alert goal line." Stances are four-point for everyone up front, splits must be exact, and we are all alert for goal-line play selections.
- Understand that the defense will have one more defender than we can block. Our wings must be on top of the MDM (most dangerous man), wing quad, and his split responsibility is critical.
- *Offensive Line and Tight End:* Alignment is on the ball. Line stances are all four-point, and our splits are six inches. Take all the ball you can get.
- *Snap Count:* We always go on *one.* Prepare to count off on a silent count, particularly on the road in crowd-noise situations. Practice the goal line with this in mind.
- *All Blockers:* Hat placement and footwork are critical. Block low to high and score with your man.
- *Running Backs:* There is no shifting unless it is called. When we shift, we have to be quick and exact.

At New England

- *Ballcarrier:* Know the blocking patterns and secure the ball.
- Goal-line offense begins and ends with the blast. We can run this play against any defense.
- Penalties and missed assignments are not tolerated. Keep your poise in the noise.
- Communication is vital. Many defenses do not give you what you worked on all week. We must be able to adjust.
- Our only goal is to score touchdowns in the goal-line situation.

When you get to the goal line, you start out with the commandments for the goal line. They are listed previously. The only time we are in a four-point stance is in short-yardage and goal-line situations. In the four-minute offense, we are in a three-point stance because we have a mixture of play-action passing and some sprint-out selections. That requires the guard to pull in some situations.

We cut the splits down to one foot in short yardage and to six inches in goal-line situations.

One thing I want to point out to you is a small point, but it was a big item to our players. Somebody is going to carry the ball, but it is no one in the offensive line. However, we will be successful if we do one thing in a goal-line situation. If the offensive block can score with his man, we will be successful. If he can block his man into the end zone, we will score. We made it a contest to see who could drive their man into the end zone. We got a little pot of money going among them and it became a competitive thing.

The defense will be in some kind of 10- or 11-man front, depending upon your formation. The ballcarrier has to BYOB (*be your own blocker*) on some defenders. We have to make sure there is no penetration and we have no missed assignments. If the offensive lineman blocks the right man, we will score down there.

I want to show you what we do in short-yardage situations. Our number-one play in short yardage is the power play (Diagram #1). I like to run this with two tight ends at the point of attack. If you do not have two tight ends, use your sixth offensive lineman at the tight end. The formation I like is the wing set with the split end set wide. We want our fastest receiver at the split end position. That way he will take the free safety out of the box. The corner does not want to cover that receiver by himself. They will give him help over the top with the free safety, and that takes him out of the box. Most defenses in short yardage are not going to vacate the middle of the field. The first front I want to show you is the bear front.

The blocking on the play is a block down and kick-out type of play. With two tight ends to the same side, we wanted to get two double-team blocks with someone coming off on a linebacker (Diagram #2). We wanted to split the defense by blocking down and kicking out. In short yardage, there is always some linebacker trying to run through a gap. We wanted to secure all gaps. We pulled the backside guard and turned him up in the hole, looking for the frontside linebacker.

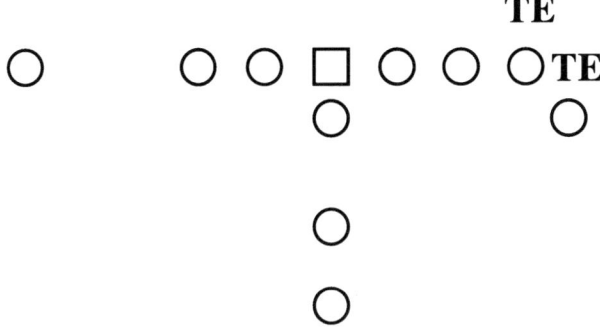

Diagram #1. Short-Yardage Formation

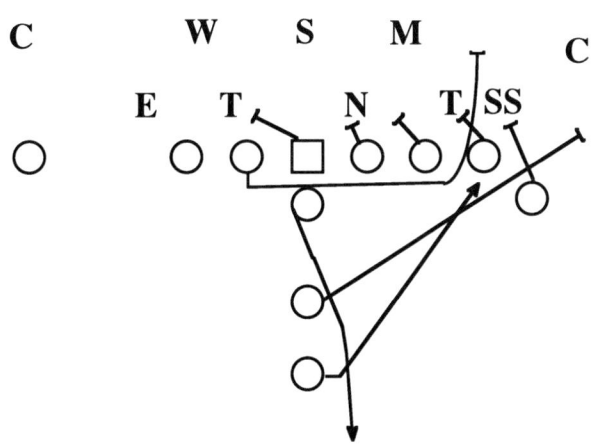

Diagram #2. Power Play

On this defense, the nose and frontside linebacker ran a stunt to the four-man side. Since this was the bear look, everyone was blocking gap assignments to the inside. The offensive guard read the outside stunt by the nose and the tackle picked him up. The guard found the blitzing linebacker and sealed the A gap. We pulled the backside guard and he turned up outside the double-team of the tight end and wing back. In this situation, the outside defenders slanted inside and the tight end and wing sealed to the inside. The fullback kicked out the first defender outside the double-team, and the pulling guard turned up in the hole for the linebacker.

This play hit one hole wider because of the bear front. This is a downhill play for the running back. He does not run the play laterally. The defense wants to force the back to run laterally, but we have to come downhill.

It did not matter what front the defense aligned in or what blitz they ran, all the gaps to the four-man side were secured. This play, for me, was the number-one play in short yardage, goal line, and four-minute offense. The lineman knew if he was uncovered, you double-teamed with someone. The philosophy of the play was to run it downhill.

You know the defense will be in some kind of eight-man front. In this formation, the defense will be a nine-man front. I like this formation because I have a four-man blocking surface. That gives me a powerside to run to. If the defense loads the box too heavily, we can hurt them with the speed receiver deep.

If the defense overloaded to the four-man side and left a three-man bubble to the split end side, we used a check-with-me call. We checked the play and ran to the split end side. The quarterback called two plays in the huddle. During the week, we gave the quarterback the premier look from the defense to the split end side. When he came to the line, if the defense gave him the premier look to the split end side, he called, "Kill, kill, and kill." That meant we ran the second play called in the huddle and we snapped the ball on one.

The power play against the 4-3 front gets a double-team between the tackle and tight end (Diagram #3). Then, one of them tries to get off the double for the backside linebacker. The wing blocks up on the Sam linebacker, and the fullback blocks the force defender to the outside. The backside guard pulls for the frontside Mike linebacker. The back runs downhill off the double-team. Wherever the crease shows up, that is where he has to get the yardage. He cannot be timid in this area. Once he sees the crease, he hits the ball downhill.

This play is the essence of the pod drill I talked about earlier. It is pad level and footwork with a lot of attitude. You have to get a double-team and secure any run-through by the linebackers. We want to double-team on the 3 technique or the

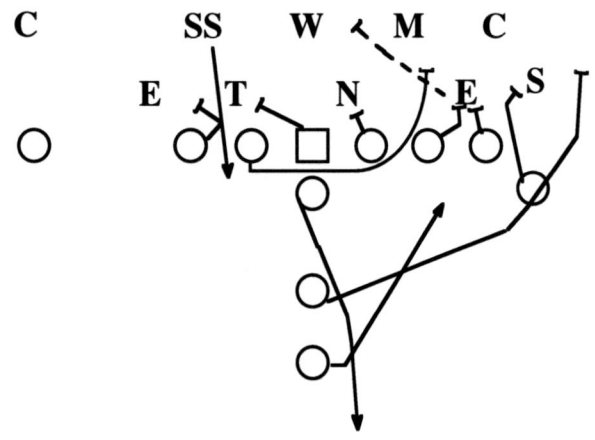

Diagram #3. Power vs. 4-3

5-technique defender. The block down and kick-out is as old as football. This type of football play goes back to Ray Crowther. It is why you spend all the time you do on sleds and boards.

I am not trying to sell you a play. You run whatever you believe in. We played the New Orleans Saints two years ago. It was fourth-and-one and we were down three points with one minute and 15 seconds to go in the game. I called this play. They knew it was coming, and we knew that I was going to call it. I think the greatest thrill in the world is running a football play where you know the defense knows what is coming and you still make the play.

Another advantage of running the same play in these situations is the feel the offensive linemen get for the defense. The offensive line begins to feel the possible adjustments the defense might make on this play. They see the same looks from the defense repeatedly, and they get used to the defense.

Against the over defense, we get two double-teams (Diagram #4). We block back on the noseguard with the center. The onside guard and tackle double on the 3-technique defender to the backside linebacker. The tight end and wing double down on the 6-technique defensive end. The

fullback leads on the force player, and the pulling guard wraps around the outside double-team for the frontside linebacker.

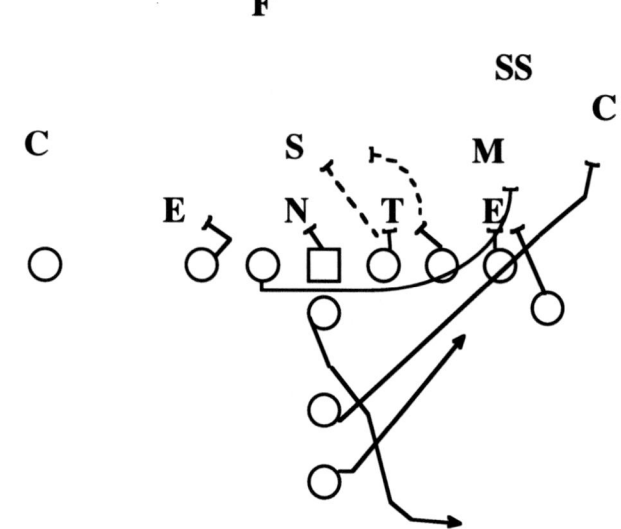

Diagram #4. Power Play vs. Over

When the defense started to pack the line of scrimmage trying to stop the off-tackle power, we had a companion play that went with the power (Diagram #5). We ran a simple toss play. We blocked down from the outside and pulled the frontside guard or tackle for the force defender. The fullback lead upfield and we were off to the races.

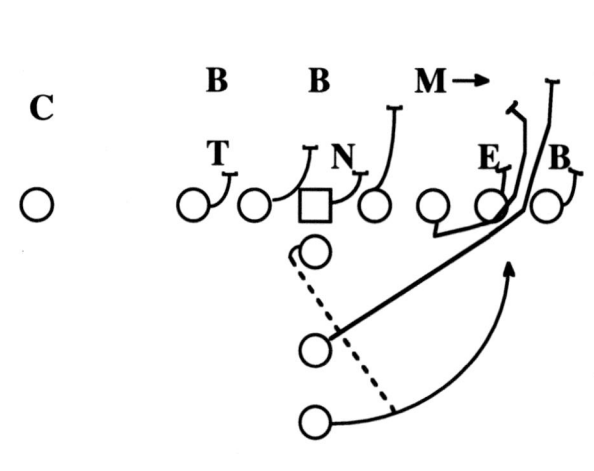

Diagram #5. Toss

The two tight ends block down to make sure the guard or tackle can pull for the force defender. The fullback is an extra blocker. The center or frontside guard has to block the middle linebacker. If they cannot get there, the fullback can pick him up.

There were two things we did that made a difference on this play (Diagram #6). In the over defense, we had a 3 technique and a 6-technique defender to the callside. In a perfect world, the two tight ends made their blocks, and the wing man chipped on the 6-technique defender, and came off to the inside linebacker. The guard reached the 3 technique, and the tackle pulled for the force. Football is not a perfect world. Teams began to tighten down with the force player in their alignment on the wing. They brought him hard from the outside hoping to jam the play.

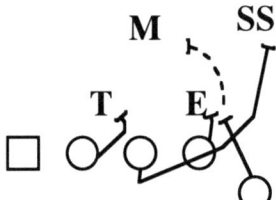

Diagram #6. Tight End/Wing Block

The rule for the two tight ends was to block the first man to their inside, on or off the line of scrimmage. The tight end has no one to his inside, and he cannot get to the linebacker, so his block became a rub block on the 6-technique defender. The tight end blocked the 6 technique, and the wing rubbed to the linebacker after chipping on the 6-technique defender. The force player was hammering us off the edge. We gave the wing the option of blocking inside or reaching the force defender.

We told the wing if the force defender aligned on him, he had the option to reach him (Diagram #7). That softens the corner for the running back and pulling lineman. The pulling tackle sees the block by the wing on the force and goes inside or outside of the block. The fullback is the extra blocker, and he or the tackle will block the inside linebacker.

The frontside guard has a reach block on the 3 technique. This play will always be a tackle pull play unless the 3 technique widens his alignment or the guard does not feel he can reach the 3-technique

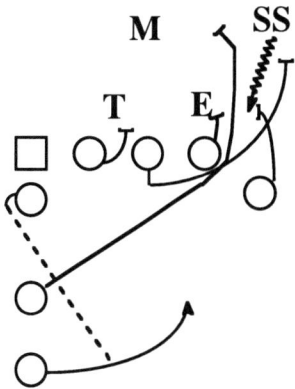

Diagram #7. Wing-Reach Block

defender. In that case, the guard can call the tackle down on the 3 technique and the guard pulls for the force. However, whenever possible, I want the tackle to pull because he can get to the edge quicker. We do not think of this play as another play. We think of it as a companion play to the power play.

The other thing I like about this play is that, in theory, you have a hat on a hat. The only player we cannot account for is the free safety. We can get a hat on everyone on the frontside of the play. The other thing you have to emphasize is the backside blocking. They have to do a hell of a job of cutting off the backside defenders. In the over defense, the backside guard has to cut off the nose tackle playing in the backside A gap.

The wing tight end wants to align as close to the tight end as the rules will allow. For us to be safe, we align the wing with his helmet on the shoulder of the tight end. I want both the tight end and the wing as close to the line of scrimmage as I can possibly get them.

Another play we ran in the short-yardage and goal-line situations was the lead play (Diagram #8). I liked to run this from a balanced two-tight-end alignment. I wanted a tight end on each side of the formation because I wanted to block the edges of the defense. From that set, we ran a downhill lead play with the fullback responsible for the first onside linebacker. On some occasions, we released the tight end to soften the edge.

I want to go back to my original premise. This is not a revolutionary play. When you play multiple

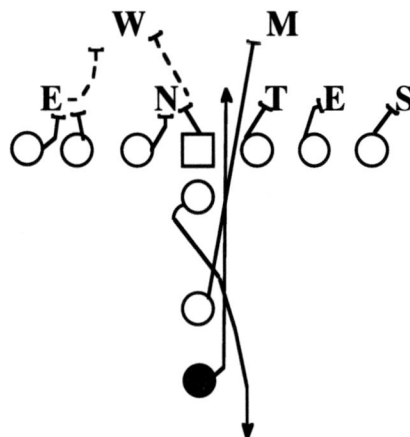

Diagram #8. Lead Play

defensive fronts, you want plays that can convert to anything the defense does. We selected plays so we could put a hat on a hat. We tell the back he is trying to get a yard. The big plays will come, but we want to get the first down.

Question: Which side do you run the play?

That is a great question. I have run it both ways. We have run it to the 3 technique. We have run it to the 1 technique so we could double the nose to the backside linebacker. If you put a gun to my head, I would rather run to the 3 technique every time. On this play, there is no offside. We do not have an offside rule. In reality, the play could go behind any of the seven linemen.

The reason I like to run it to the 3 technique is it gives definition to the fullback and running back as to where the hole will be. The 3 technique has responsibility for the B gap and will charge outside the guard. There is no question where the fullback has to run.

The problem with running to the bubble is the linebacker. You have a better angle on the nose and backside linebacker, and you can get a double-team on the 7 technique on the inside shoulder of the tight end. The problem is you turn the linebacker into a kamikaze defender. When he sees the guard block down, he meets the fullback in the backfield. I like to give the fullback some breathing room so when he gets to the line of scrimmage he can adjust. We have

a commitment to this football play because it adapts. I hope that answers your question.

We want plays where you can come off the line and move the line of scrimmage. We want plays that adapt to whatever the defense has to offer. The lead and power play are the heart of what we do.

We have a companion play for this play also. Every coach in this room knows the linebackers are keying the fullback. They know the fullback will take them to every play we have. We put in this play to help the lead play. This is the poor man's counter play, which I call a *bend* (Diagram #9). The callside tight end releases and blocks the MDM to the outside. The callside tackle and guard are responsible for the 7 technique and the Will linebacker.

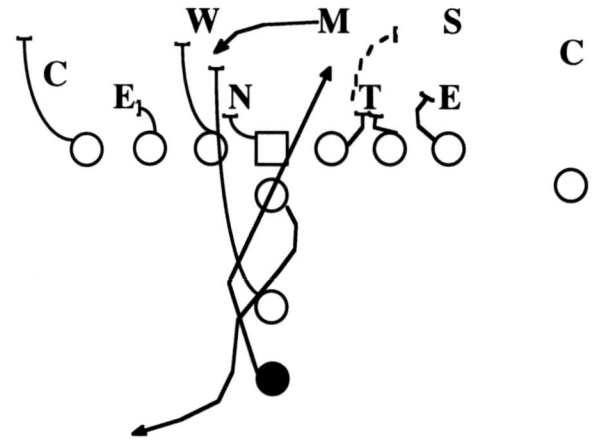

Diagram #9. Bend

The center puts his helmet in the nape of the nose tackle's neck. I want to give the nose the illusion that the center is trying to reach him. The backside guard and tackle run a zone combination block for the 3 technique and the Mike linebacker. The backside tight end cuts off the 7-technique defender. The fullback is going to block the Mike linebacker as he flows over the top to get to the play. This play is a poor man's counter play. You run a counter without pulling anyone. The running back starts to the callside and bends the ball back to the backside. All we have done on the play is change the assignment between the fullback and the guard.

The guard takes on the Will linebacker, and the fullback blocks the Mike linebacker.

In the short-yardage offense, we needed something that was a change of pace. We were starting to get a lot of the bear front. We wanted a speed break. We wanted to come to the line of scrimmage in an unusual formation and do something quick. We decided to do it against Carolina because they were our big rivals.

We came out of the huddle and hustled to the line of scrimmage (Diagram #10). We had an additional tackle in the game and aligned him in the backfield in the guard-and-tackle gap. We ran the fullback dive play to the four-man side. The extra lineman came out of the huddle a fraction of a second late. He looked like he was going to align on the line of scrimmage, and Carolina did not pay much attention to him.

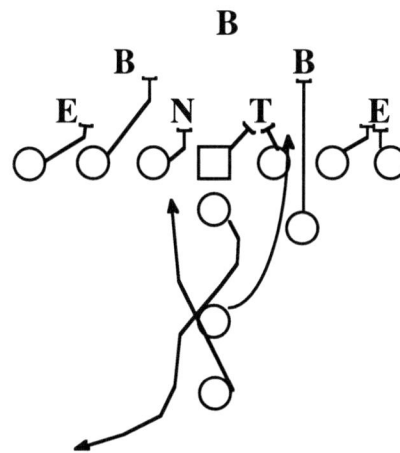

Diagram #10. Tackle lead

The offensive line aligned with a six-inch split instead of one foot. The extra tackle aligned one yard off the line of scrimmage. We snapped the ball immediately and ran the fullback dive up the right check of the right offensive guard. We doubled inside and outside the hole and isolated the linebacker with the extra lineman. We used the speed break and got surge from the offensive line and got the yard we needed. This is not a bad idea and it certainly is not original.

Years ago, I saw the University of Mississippi do something like this. I thought it was interesting. I keep a notebook of interesting ideas, and I was looking for something that was different. We practiced it and used it in the game. We huddled five yards off the ball and had one word for the play. We called, "Fire." I told the tackle to run through the B gap and block any opposite color in the hole.

We ran the play three times in the Carolina game and went three for three in first downs. People began to prepare for it so I had another thought. I put an additional lineman in the game. Instead of aligning on one side, we aligned on both sides with the extra linemen. I had seven offensive linemen in the game. That is all we carry on the team.

We are seeing more of a 46 defense in the short-yardage situations (Diagram #11). Teams get into this defense because they do not think they can stop the quarterback sneak. If they cannot stop the quarterback sneak, they will not be able to stop the fullback dive. I worked all week long preparing the offensive tackle and guards to knock the crap out of the 3-technique defenders. We wanted to see how far we could drive them off the ball. The center had one job. He could not get backed up. He had to hold the fort.

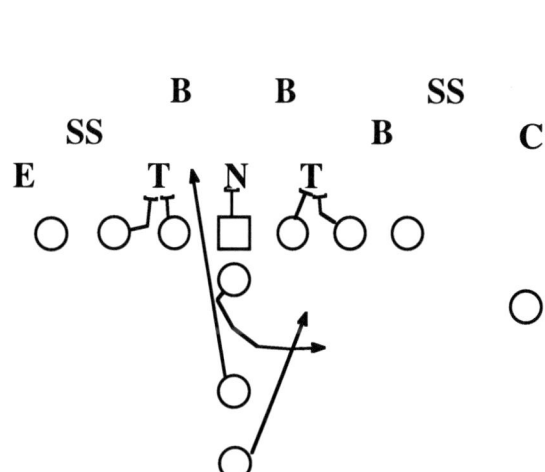

Diagram #11. Fullback Dive vs. 46

That is not much of a play, but that is all we want. We want to run for one yard. It keeps the offense on the field for at least another series. It does not take away from what we are doing. The main course of our short-yardage offense is the power play.

We modified the speed-break play and ran a power-I set with a split end. We ran the isolation play and the fullback dive from that formation. The next time we played Carolina, we added a wrinkle to the power-I set. Against them earlier, we ran the dive with the extra lineman and they had seen the power-I set, so we decided to run the dive away from the power back (Diagram #12). The backside 3 technique slanted to the power back, and the backside end spiked down the line of scrimmage. The fullback got too wide on the play, and the tackle got off balance and could not make the block. We made the first down but did not have the success we had hoped for.

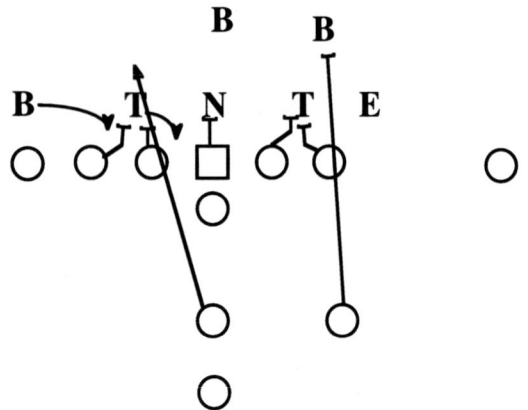

Diagram #12. Fullback Dive Away

That is our philosophy behind the short-yardage play. We use the power and the lead as our main staple plays. The two companion plays are good, and the dives have been successful. The dive last year was a nice added play for us.

In the goal-line situation, we liked the idea of the dive. We have seen a lot of what we call 53 jam and the 46 defense in the goal-line situation. We started running the dive against those defenses. With the multiple fronts being run in the NFL, we have watched and studied other people to see what is successful for them. Do not change for the sake of changing, but sometimes there is merit to what they are doing and you might want to change what you are doing.

For the last three or four years, I have been watching the Patriots, and they look like they have one play they run the majority of the time in these situations. It is nothing more than an outside zone play. They have a couple of different ways to block it. We decided that was a play we wanted to add into our goal-line offense.

Against the 53 jam in the goal line, we like to run the dive inside the two-yard line (Diagram #13). When we get inside the two-yard line, I like to run the dive. I would not run it outside the two, but it is good for a yard. It is muscle ball when you run this play. You do not need a bunch of moving parts on the one-yard line. We get to the line, get set, and run the play on one. The first thing I look at is the depth of the middle linebacker.

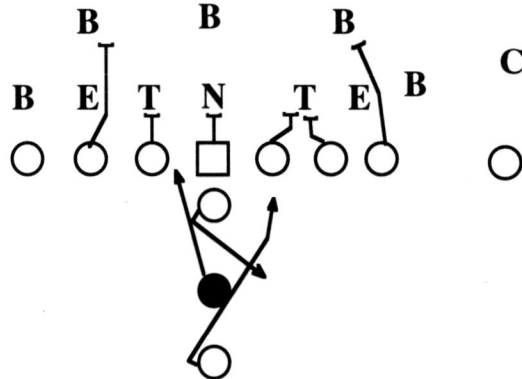

Diagram #13. Goal-Line Dive

The left guard has a defensive tackle aligned on his inside eye. He blocks down on him. The left tackle has a tight 5 technique on his outside with a linebacker stack behind him. The tackle wants to fire inside the 5 technique and rub block to the linebacker. We double-team the 3-technique tackle to the other side. The center has to hold the fort. He cannot get back up off the line of scrimmage by the nose. With the depth of the middle linebacker, we feel we can double and hit the blast before he can get to the line of scrimmage.

If the defense is a 62 with double A-gap defenders, we pick out one of those defenders and double him. The center and onside guard double the A-gap defender to that side. The backside guard has to do a hell of a job of getting off the ball because with the double-team on the other side, there will be a void over the center and he has to knock the defender back off the ball. He does not want to cutoff block on the defender. He wants to get his hat on the inside thigh pad of the defender and drive him over the pile. We run the tailback on a counter move to the backside to seal any penetration from that side.

When the linebackers begin to move up on the line of scrimmage, we cannot run the dive play. We run the stretch play like the New England Patriots. I like this play because you can run it to the wing or away from the wing. You can put the wing in motion and run toward the motion or away from the motion. It is an adaptable play in the goal-line situation. It is one of our core plays in the goal-line offense.

One of the things we spend a lot of time on each week is self-scouting. If you do not do that, I think you should. You have to know what formation you are running and you need to know what you are doing. If you use motion, are you running toward it or away from it? The back carrying the ball is not important. In this situation, you will give the ball to your touchdown maker. The self-scouting gave us two things. It gave us the ability to disguise what we were doing. The defense could never track whether we were running to the motion or away from it. The second thing was we did not care what the front was.

The blocking on this play was zone blocking (Diagram #14). The decision has to be made with the tight end and tackle to the callside. The tight end and tackle will combo on the 9-technique end. The tight end and tackle use a combo block for the 9-technique end and outside linebacker. However, if the linebacker walks up on the line of scrimmage, the end reaches the 9 technique, and the tackle reaches the linebacker. The onside guard reaches the 3 technique.

The center, backside guard, and tackle are responsible for the nose, middle linebacker, and backside 3 technique. This is a tough block if the middle linebacker walks up into the line of scrimmage on the callside. The fullback blocks the

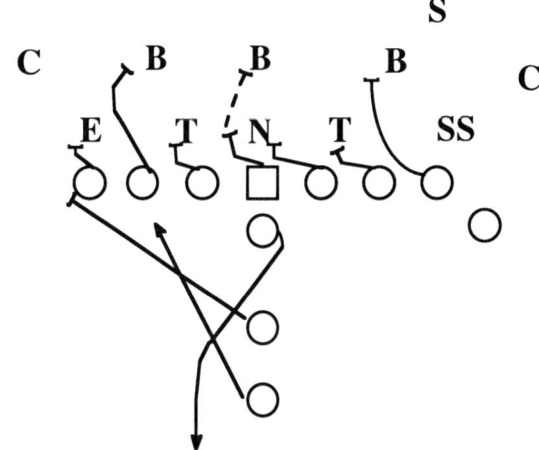

Diagram #14. Stretch

force defender. If we run the play away from the wing, the fullback has to know whether the force is an on-the-line player or off-the-line player.

The fullback's landmark is the defender's outside thigh pad. That causes the defender to widen, and we can get inside of him. If he does not widen, the running back should have the corner. As he takes his first step, he has to read the block of the defensive end on his defender. The defender may loop to the outside and force the X's defender on an inside stunt.

The quarterback did not open to the play, unlike most stretch plays. We reversed out to get the ball to the running back. Our thinking was to slow down the running back. We did not want the running back to be a true outside stretch runner. We wanted him to read the outside combination block. We wanted the angle of the running back to be the inside leg of the tight end and not wider.

The coaching point for the running back is where the free hitters are coming from. We cannot get to the backside linebacker on the play. The running back must know who he is so he does not take a big hit from someone he does not see. That goes with the idea of ball security in this area. If he takes an inside cut, he has to expect a big hit from the inside and protect the ball accordingly.

When we brought the wing in motion, we did not want him to have and inside-out angle on the outside defender. If we got inside out on the force defender, he squeezed the hole, and that is not what we wanted. We wanted his landmark to be head-up the outside defender. If the outside defender stepped outside, it was all right to pin the defender. By making the defender step outside, we widened the hole for the running back. If we ran the play to the motion, the fullback was track blocking. He came off the butt of the tight end and blocked whatever showed up.

The tailback takes an open step. His next step is toward the outside leg of the tackle. We do not want the tailback to get too wide too fast. If he does, he cannot take advantage of the off-tackle read. I always felt, if the defense crashed the corner or we hooked the corner, you had enough speed to get to the corner of the end zone.

The last thing I leave you with is this. A number of years ago I coached the New York Jets. I happened to be in New York the second week of the season. The infamous 9/11 attacks struck that day. I remember sitting in my office and one of the assistants came in and told me to turn on the TV. He said a plane just hit the World Trade Center. I had a daughter who worked in that area and I was concerned about it. I turned the TV on just in time to see the second plane hit the building.

A week later, the Jets and Giants agreed to go down on buses to the site of the World Trade Center and work in the disaster center. They would work for the Red Cross or the cantina and do whatever they could in that moment of need. When we got down there, it was a devastating scene. One of the fellas that worked in our locker room happened to be a New York City fireman. Life magazine put a book out with pictures of the disaster in it. One of the things that stuck out in my mind was a picture of this fella who worked in our locker room going up the steps in the Trade Center with about 70 pounds of equipment.

You could see his eyes were as big as saucers. People were running down past him in obvious panic. These firemen were going up the steps. It kind of blew me away.

I asked him about a year later how he could do that. There were two buildings on fire, people were panicking, and you grabbed your gear and ran into the building. He told me it was simple. He said, "Bill, all the men on that truck train every day as a team. It does not matter if we are called to get a cat out of a tree. When the wagon pulls up, every man on that truck has a job. Every man on the wagon knows that the man on either side of him depends on him doing his job. I was scared, but I knew if I did not go into the building with them, they could not do their jobs and they would not make it out alive." Even today, when I talk about it, I get goose bumps on the back of my neck.

I say to you, if you are a head coach, that is what you should be trying to get done on your staff. If you are a position coach, that is damn sure what you are selling in your room. I am not trying to compare the two situations as equal. What I am trying to tell you is the philosophy is the same. If you are coaching offensive line, you, as a group, are as good as the five players that work together. If you can sell the idea that all the offensive linemen are necessary parts to one unit, you will be successful. All the components of the unit and for the unit to be successful means everyone has to do his job.

That goes back to what I said. You are what you are on film. You tell them that from the get-go. If you know who to block and you are trying to block him the right way, that is all we can ask. With that, I leave you. Thank you for your time.

ABOUT THE AUTHOR

Owning 44 years of coaching expertise, Bill Muir is entering his 32nd NFL season and will coach the Chiefs' offensive line in 2009. This respected coach came to Kansas City after spending seven seasons as the offensive coordinator/offensive line coach for Tampa Bay (2002 to 2008).

During his tenure in Tampa Bay, Muir was part of a staff that helped guide the Buccaneers to a victory in Super Bowl XXXVII in 2002. Thanks to his offensive units, the Buccaneers also claimed NFC South crowns in both 2005 and 2007. Despite boasting one of the league's youngest offensive fronts in 2007, quarterback Jeff Garcia earned a Pro-Bowl berth, and the Buccaneers scored 334 points, the fourth-highest seasonal total in team history.

Recognized for consistently developing some of the NFL's best offensive fronts, Muir's blocking unit paved the way for running back Cadillac Williams, who earned NFL Rookie of the Year honors in 2005. In 2003, the Buccaneers ranked 10th in the NFL in total offense as quarterback Brad Johnson set single-season franchise records with 354 completions and 26 touchdowns.

Muir spent seven seasons as the offensive line coach with the New York Jets (1995 to 2001), where he began his association with Chiefs general manager Scott Pioli and head coach Todd Haley. Under his jurisdiction in 2000, the Jets allowed 20.0 sacks, tying for the lowest total in the NFL.

Running back Curtis Martin posted four 1,000-yard seasons during Muir's tenure in New York, including a team-record 1,513 yards in 2001 as Martin earned his fourth Pro-Bowl nod. The Jets were fourth in the NFL in rushing in 2001, averaging 128.4 rushing yards per game, the club's best ranking since 1991.

Muir spent three campaigns as the offensive line coach for Philadelphia (1992 to 1994). Thanks to his offensive front, the Eagles ranked ninth in the NFL, averaging 110.1 rushing yards per game in 1994. He joined the Eagles after a three-year stint with Indianapolis (1989 to 1991). He served two seasons as the Colts' defensive coordinator before assuming the post of assistant head coach/offensive line coach in 1991. Muir spent four seasons as the of-fensive line coach for Detroit (1985 to 1988) after serving in the same capacity with New England (1982 to 1984).

The Pittsburgh, Pennsylvania native began his first tour of duty in Tampa Bay as a member of the person-nel department. He worked as a scout in 1978 before serving as a pro scout from 1979 to 1981. The Buccaneers advanced to the postseason in 1979 and 1981, including a berth in the 1979 NFC Championship game, a remarkable feat for a franchise that began playing just three seasons earlier in 1976.

Prior to entering the NFL ranks, Muir spent two seasons coaching the offensive line at Southern Methodist University (1976 to 1977). He served in the same capacity with the World Football League's Houston/Shreveport Steamers (1974 to 1975). Muir enjoyed a stint as defensive coordinator at Idaho State University (1972 to 1973), in addition to coaching the defensive line and working as defensive coordinator at Rhode Is-land (1970 to 1971).

From 1968 to 1969, Muir was the offensive line coach for the Orlando Panthers of the fledgling Continental Football League that fielded teams from 1965 to 1969. Muir was part of an Orlando staff that won the 1968 league title game. Muir's first two coaching assignments were coaching the offensive and defensive lines at Delaware Valley College (1966 to 1967) and Susquehanna University (1965). A standout tackle at Susquehanna from 1962 to 1964, Muir was inducted into the school's Hall of Fame in 1990 after being named to the school's "Top 100" players of all time.

Born in Pittsburgh, Pennsylvania, Muir graduated from Susquehanna University with a B.A. in 1965. Muir and his wife, Barbara have two children, Keelan and Brady, and five grandchildren.

MUIR AT A GLANCE

- 2009: Kansas City Chiefs, Offensive Line Coach
- 2002-2008: Tampa Bay Buccaneers, Offensive Coordinator/Offensive Line Coach
- 1995-2001: New York Jets, Offensive Line Coach
- 1992-1994: Philadelphia Eagles, Offensive Line Coach
- 1991: Indianapolis Colts, Assistant Head Coach/Offensive Line Coach
- 1989-1990: Indianapolis Colts, Defensive Coordinator
- 1985-1988: Detroit Lions, Offensive Line Coach
- 1982-1984: New England Patriots, Offensive Line Coach
- 1978-1981: Tampa Bay Buccaneers, Pro Scout
- 1976-1977: SMU, Offensive Line Coach
- 1974-1975: Houston/Shreveport (WFL), Offensive Line Coach
- 1972-1973: Idaho State University, Defensive Coordinator
- 1970-1971: Rhode Island, Defensive Coordinator/Defensive Line Coach
- 1968-1969: Orlando (Continental League) Offensive Line
- 1966-1967: Delaware Valley College, Offensive/Defensive Line Coach
- 1965: Susquehanna University, Offensive/Defensive Line Coach

OFFENSIVE LINE PASS FUNDAMENTALS

University of Georgia

Thank you. It is an honor to be here representing the University of Georgia and Coach Mark Richt. I have been fortunate to have been around a lot of good football coaches in my career. I can start with my high school coach in Jim Resita at Trion High School in Georgia, and Neil Callaway who was my coach at Auburn University. I have learned from Larry Beightol, Larry Zierlein, Jerry Sandusky, and a few other coaches like those. I have tried to take something from every one of those coaches.

The first thing we start with is our pass-set drills. We do a lot of these drills in the first five minutes of practice. Our head coach handles the quarterback and center exchange. On day one of spring practice and day one of fall practice, we teach the fundamentals of the passing game.

I heard Coach Paul Alexander of the Bengals say that most sacks come from not covering the defender up. We try to cover everyone up. We teach two sets. They are the *post set* and the *kick set*. On the post set, it is a slide-inside set. The relationship we want to get is where the outside eye is on his inside eye. We want to cover the man up.

In the drill, we have four blockers with a defender covering them. We take a slide-inside step. We do not want to float on the first step. First, on our left tackle and left guard we have the defenders head-up. Then, we have them shade to our left. We want to get to a point where our outside eye is on his inside eye. We are almost in the correct position already. We take a slight kick outside, but holding our weight inside.

On the side of the right tackle and guard, we have the defenders lined up on the inside. If I tell them I want their outside eye on his inside eye, to do that, he has to cover a lot of ground. So, basically, if the defender is lined up inside, we tell our linemen to get nose to nose with the defender.

On our left side, we are kicking and carrying our weight on the inside. On the right side, we are working to get nose to nose (Diagram #1).

Diagram #1. Pass-Set Drills

Then, we shade to the other side. Now, on the right side, we are kicking, and on the left side, we are post cutting. You can do these simple drills the first two minutes of practice.

Our next drill is the *hand replace drill.* We can do this drill when the centers are doing their snaps. We line up with the defender in front of us and we just replace our hands on his front pads. He knocks them off, but we replace them repeatedly.

We want to get the feel for replacing the hands as quickly as we can. Then, we change up the defense. I will tell the defender to rip to the inside. Your hands are moving, moving, and then you have to replace them and get a good punch. We punch the defender down inside, and then we kick back with depth. This stimulates a defender going inside on a twist; we punch him down, and then we come off on the defender coming around the block.

It can simulate a fire-zone blitz with the tackle going outside and the linebacker coming inside on the blitz. We push off down inside, and then we work to get depth. The point I am making is that you can incorporate several drills to get more out of the reps.

From there, we go to our *hats-off rush*. I learned this drill several years ago. When I was a senior at Auburn University, I used to duck my head a lot. I would headbutt the defender. The seniors would shave the heads of the freshmen. This one kid got mad at me because I shaved his head. The coach told me to take my helmet off and let the freshman come at me full speed. I had to take my helmet off, and that is where I got the name of this drill.

I am fortunate at Georgia because the first 15 to 20 minutes of practice is special teams work. I have all five of our interior linemen to work on pass protection and pass progression blocking. We are going to do four drills. We do the *mirror, bull, push-pull,* and the *combo* drill. These are all movement drills.

A coaching point on the mirror drill is to break down like a linebacker, with the chest over the knees and the knees over the toes. We want to get big eyes on the target. We want them to pick out a small spot on the defender. I heard a coach a few years ago speak at this clinic and all he talked about was the eyes. At the time, I did not see how important the eyes were in blocking. Now, I am seeing more and more why the eyes are so important in blocking. We pick out a small target on his number and keep the eyes on that target.

In the mirror drill, we want to shuffle. The definition is this. If my right foot goes six inches, then my left foot must go six inches. We want our feet tight to the ground. We do not take a lead step. We want to press off the back foot. We do not want to click our heels together. We want a wide base. We want to stick the foot into the ground when they get to the cone or as the defender changes direction. We press back off and go the other way as the defender changes directions. It is like ice skating in that we want to press off the back foot. That is the mirror drill. Everyone does this drill.

Next is the bull drill. What we are trying to do is to strike with our hands. We want to keep our head out of the block. We do not want to be headbutting. We do not want to duck on the block. It is a drill we can do fast. The inside hands are going to win on this drill.

Coach Alexander talked about the push-pull drill. It is especially good for kids just coming out of high school. At this level, most of them do not have great body control. This drill teaches body control. What the drill does for us is this: Can the man coming off the block bull rush us and then snatch the blocker as he goes by him? You must have some core strength to run this drill. This is a good way to train for it here. This is how I teach the drill. I tell the players they have a telephone pole down the center of their bodies. When the defender bulls you, we want the blocker to sink his butt and give ground begrudingly. When he pulls you, you are going to walk back up into the defender with tight feet.

We tell the defender to put his right hand on the neck and the left hand on the blocker's shoulder, and apply steady pressure as he retreats back and forth. It is an offensive drill, and this is true with young guys. We do not want the defenders to "rag doll" with the blockers. Some of the older players will do that with the young players because they do not have a clue what is going on. We want steady pressure—push, pull. The blocker gets the feel of the drill so he can walk up into the defender with tight feet.

We want our players to be strong. It is a matter of being solid. It is having that telephone pole right down the center of your body.

After this, we put it all together with a combo block. We do all four of the drills including the mirror, bull, push-pull, and the combo.

We start out by telling the players it is play-action and we are going to jump the defender. The man grabs outside, then side to side, and backward and forward. I want to control the drill offensively. If the defender is going to the blocker's right side, he should get strong with his right hand. If he is going to the left, get strong with the left hand. We want the blocker to control the defender. We want the defensive man to grab the shoulders and take off, make the blocker move his feet and throw him off balance.

Later in the spring, we do the same drills, but we incorporate the twist with the drill. When we work on the drills, we want to shoot our hands inside, and we want to be strong inside. Coach Whitworth told me if the defensive man gives you a chance, you should grab it. I thought that was a good coaching point.

That is our movement part of our pass protection. Then, we get into the punch part of the block. What we are trying to do here is teach the initial punch. In our pass protection, we want to stop their initial charge and make the defender start over again.

We break down like a linebacker. We put our hands up, and the defender walks up to a position where we can make our block. The defender must hold the dummy tight against his chest or the drill does not work very well. We start out by pushing off, and then we want to jackhammer the defender. You can tell if the blocker is doing a good job or not by watching the defender's head. If he is doing the block right, that head will pop up as the blocker makes contact.

After we punch the defender, we reset and strike the defender. We want to strike with our hands at 60 percent to 90 percent. Our hands are up high on the dummy. We do not want to lock our arms all the way out. We want the arms extended from 60 percent to 90 percent. We push the defender away, and then restrike him as he continues the rush. Again, here we are just teaching the initial strike. We want to stop the charge by the defender and make him start all over. We punch and we grab. A coaching point is this: If the blocker is blocking correctly, you should never see his elbows.

I was a rookie at San Diego in 1988. For two weeks, I did not block a defender. I knew I was about to get fired. The scout who convinced the Chargers to draft me came up to me and said, "We both are about to get fired. I have an idea I want to discuss with you. You need to learn how to pass block. I have a sledgehammer in my hand. I want you to get down in your stance. When I say set, hike, you react. I am going to knock your head off."

What do you do when someone is going to hit you with a sledgehammer? You get your hands up in front of your face. I have good feet. I know coaches preach low hands, but I had not figured it out at that time. I could move my feet, but my hands were down around my waist and I could never get my hands on anyone, so I was not blocking anyone.

After that experience, we started doing a drill to make the blocker get his hands up. We do two from a two-point stance and two from a three-point stance or a down stance. We give the defender a hand dummy. I tell him to use it as if it was a Louisville Slugger™ baseball bat, and knock his head off. The defender takes the dummy and whacks the blocker in the helmet. A good way to check the blockers set is to call, "Set," and strike the blocker at the same time.

With the center, he has to learn to kick both ways. We will do two for him on each side. We made a tape of these drills for every high school in the country. The Army made the film and distributed it for us.

The next drill is *kick the boards*. One of the big problems we have with tackles, or other offensive linemen, is that they open their hips or they turn their shoulders on the block. They are not semisquare to the line of scrimmage. Some quarterbacks get the ball away fast and that helps the blockers. If you have a quarterback who likes to hold the ball and pump it several times, you must hold that block longer. If we can get our blockers to get three good kicks on the pass block with the shoulders semisquare, we have a chance to be successful on the protection. This is just a training tool primarily for the tackles (Diagram #2). We have the boards at an angle. The blockers retreat three steps, keeping their feet spread on the board. We do the drill from the up stance and the down stance. We stress pushing off with the inside foot on this drill.

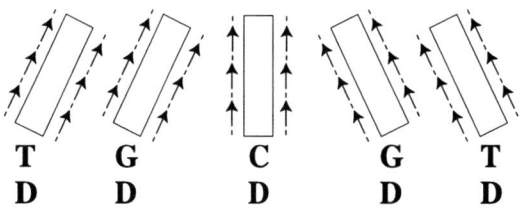

Drill #2. Board Drill, Three Kicks

We want to see the inside foot tight to the ground. We want them to press off with the inside foot and to carry the weight inside.

We want to take it one step farther. Now we work on the offside rush. When we teach this drill, we want the defender to put his foot on the line. It screws up the drill if he is too far back or too close. We have our blocker with his far foot on the line. All we want the defender to do is to grab the back number and clear his hip. The blocker wants to explode back carrying his weight inside. I tell the defender we want him to stab the blocker's back number. We do two from the up position and two from the down position.

We take the drill to the next step, which is the offside and the counter. When the defender comes across the blocker's face, he must counter the move by getting the farside hand, striking the defender, and squaring his shoulders. We talk about the fact that the closer the defender is, the tighter the set. If we are in a full slide, the drill will work.

That is our base fundamental pass move. We have other drills we use as well. Just like the other drills we discussed, when the center and quarterback are working on the exchange, we can work any of the other drills we have discussed.

I have some film clips that I want to go over. We had a walk-on center come to camp last year. He kicked the crap out of everyone. He started 12 out of 13 games for us. This spring, he got in a bad habit of not using his off hand when he made contact on the defender. I told him to use his off hand and to knock the crap out of the nose man. When he started using his off hand on the rusher, he was amazed at the difference in his block. That is a tip that is good for the center.

The next clips are shots of our blockers getting their hands inside on the blocks. One point on the bull drill is that we want the blocker to give ground begrudgingly.

When we run the play-action pass, we want the line to jump on the defender as quickly as possible. We want to block the defender high.

I hope these drills will help you, especially those of you that are just getting started in coaching. Starting out as a coach, you need a base set of drills that you can do every day. This is what we do and it works for us, and I hope it will work for you.

High school coaches make a big impact on the young people. I have the utmost respect for my high school line coach. Keep doing the job you are doing. I appreciate your attention.

ABOUT THE AUTHOR

Stacy Searels was named the offensive line coach for the University of Georgia Bulldogs in January, 2007, after serving four years coaching the offensive line at Louisiana State University, during which time the Tigers won a national championship (2003), one SEC title (2003), and two SEC East titles (2003 and 2005). He added the duties of running game coordinator in 2009.

A native of Trion, Georgia and a 1990 graduate of Auburn University, Searels was an All-American lineman for the Tigers in 1987 when he was a teammate of current Georgia defensive line coach Rodney Garner. Prior to joining the LSU staff, he coached the offensive line at the University of Cincinnati (2000 to 2002), Appalachian State University (1994 to 2000), and served as a graduate assistant at Auburn (1992 to 1993).

Searels made a habit of producing All-American linemen for LSU. He coached two first-team All-Americans in Stephen Peterman and Ben Wilkerson and a second-team All-American in Andrew Whitworth. Five of his Tiger linemen earned spots on NFL rosters. In addition, during that four-year stretch, LSU's offensive line produced a pair of first-team Academic All-Americans in Rodney Reed and Rudy Niswanger. LSU had an offensive lineman named first-team Academic All-American four straight years. Niswanger became the most decorated student-athlete in school history in 2005, winning the Draddy Award as college football's top scholar-athlete as well as being the inaugural recipient of the Wuerffel Trophy.

Searels joined the staff at LSU after a two-year stint as offensive line coach at Cincinnati. During his two-year stay with the Bearcats, Cincinnati played in two bowl games as well as winning the school's first conference title since 1964 by capturing the 2002 Conference USA crown. In 2002, Searels coached an offensive line that helped Cincinnati lead Conference USA in total offense (397.5 yards per game), while averaging 29.2 points a contest.

Prior to joining Cincinnati, Searels served as an assistant coach at Appalachian State from 1994 to 2000, helping the I-AA squad to five playoff appearances and to a pair of Southern Conference titles. While at Appalachian State, Searels was presented with the NCAA Award of Valor, which has only been awarded eight times since its inception in 1974 and honors those who "when confronted with a situation involving personal danger, averted or minimized potential disaster by courageous action or noteworthy bravery." He was recognized for his act of courage following a head-on collision involving a van carrying members of the Mountaineer football team and support staff on September 30, 2000.

Searels got his start in coaching as a graduate assistant at Auburn in 1992, working with the Tiger squad that posted a perfect 11-0 mark in 1993.

As a senior, in 1987, Searels earned first-team All-American honors from both the Associated Press and Football News. Searels was a three-year starter for Auburn, blocking for Heisman Trophy winner Bo Jackson in 1985 and All-American Brent Fullwood in 1986. He also participated in four bowls.

A first-team All-Southeastern Conference selection as both a junior and senior, he was honored with the team's Ken Rice Award as the school's best blocking lineman in 1987. He played in both the Japan Bowl and the Senior Bowl following the 1987 season. In 1990, the Birmingham Post-Herald named Searels to the Auburn team of the 1980s.

Searels was a fourth-round draft pick by the San Diego Chargers in 1988, playing two seasons there before moving to the Miami Dolphins for the 1990 season. He ended his professional career in 1991 with the New York/New Jersey Knights of the World League of American Football.

Searels graduated from Auburn with a degree in marketing and transportation in 1990. He followed that with a master's degree in higher education administration from Auburn in 1995. Searels is married to the former Patricia Hale and the couple has two daughters, Taylor and Savannah.

SEARELS AT A GLANCE

- 2009-present: University of Georgia, Run Game Coordinator/Offensive Line Coach
- 2007-2008: University of Georgia, Offensive Line Coach
- 2003-2006: Louisiana State University, Offensive Line Coach
- 2000-2002: University of Cincinnati, Offensive Line Coach
- 1994-2000: Appalachian State University, Offensive Line Coach
- 1992-1993: Auburn University, Graduate Assistant

DRILLS AND LINE BLOCKING SCHEMES/THE STEELERS' DRAW PLAY

Pittsburgh Steelers

I appreciate that introduction from Bob Wylie. However, he left a few things out of my bio. I started out coaching as a high school coach. I do not know how many of you are high school coaches, but I want you to know that I understand your situation. I do appreciate being here and I consider it an honor to speak here today.

I am going to get started talking about some of the things we do in working with offensive linemen. I hope I can give you an idea on some techniques and drills, and possibly give you some tips on how to organize your practices and to help you become better organized in what you do in your offense.

We are an inside zone and gap-running team. By gap, I am referring to lead-type running plays where we block back, etc. We have some plays where we pull the guard and some plays where we do not pull the guard. All of the individual drills I do in the running game are suited for those types of plays.

Footwork is vital in technique. Your feet put your body where it needs to be to get the job done that you are trying to do. In all of our drills, we are trying to teach through the drill the technique necessary to use on each move. We said the feet put your body where it needs to be to become better at whatever you are trying to do. In all of our drills, we are trying to teach through the drill the technique, with the primary emphasis on the footwork.

We have all heard Bob Wylie talk about the squares in lining up for drills. We do not use squares. We have about 10 players that work with the offensive line. We just stagger them out in doing our drills. We may have one player on the goal line and one player on the five-yard line, and we stagger across the field with the players we are working

with. It is the same idea that Bob has talked about over the years.

The first thing we do is teach the base block. Everything we do, as far as footwork is concerned, is a one-two movement. It is foot up, foot down. We start out with the players we are working with lined up in a staggered alignment. We have five groups of two men working together. We can do the drills one at a time or we can do them as a group (Diagram #1). It depends on our time allotment for that period. During the spring and minicamps, we have them lined up, and we go one at a time. I want to see all of the players, so I do them one at a time. As we progress into the season, then we have them go as a group.

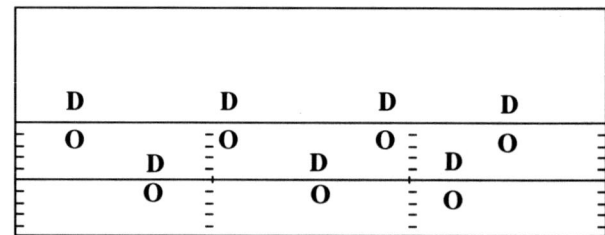

Diagram #1. Group Alignment

All of the things I am going to talk about here today are going to take about five minutes for the players to do. First, we take our tackle that is trying to get a base block on a defender that is lined up slightly to the outside (Diagram #2). We want two things in these drills. These steps are vital in this block. First, we want to pick the outside foot up and set it in the ground. We want the step to be a settle step. We want the second step to be a short step toward the middle of the defender. We want him to plant it in the ground flat-footed and gain some ground. If he takes a long step on the second step, he cannot stay with the defender.

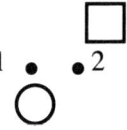

Diagram #2. Two Steps/Outside Block

The player does not have to be fast into the block. He can get his feet up and down, and he has time to take the second step in the ground. He keeps his hands inside. He gets into a power-base position.

This is the first thing we do with our offensive linemen. We work against the defender when he is slightly outside and then again when he is inside. We go one man at a time, and then we go with the entire group working on the drill. We can do this drill with five blockers at a time in a matter of a few minutes. We work on the different blocks we need to work on for a particular type of play. We can work on all footwork in this simple drill.

When we get into the game films, we want to see that the techniques used in the games are the same as we use in our drills. The first step is the settle step up and down. The second step is up in a leverage position. We want the blocker in a hit-and-leverage position. We do not want him to be in a hurry. We would like the blockers to stay flat-footed. They get up on their toes at times, but we want them to keep their feet up and under their bodies. It is hard to get movement at any level of the game but especially at this level. If you have a good base and you have leverage, you can move the defenders when you make contact.

We do not want our blocker to try to fly through the defender. He makes contact, lifts, and drives the defender back.

The second thing we do is a base block versus one man removed from the blocker. Let's say we are running the Bob play or we are running the one-back zone play. All of the drills we are doing here are inside-zone drills. We do not run the outside zone, so I am not showing any reach blocks on the 3 technique or anything like that. This is just as if we would run the inside zone to the openside.

This is a 1-on-1 block. It could be a right tackle on the defensive end (Diagram #3). If the defense knows we are going to run in this area, they are going to pinch, scrape, and come inside to try to jam the hole. The blocker must be under control as he comes off the line.

The first step is an open step with the near foot. The second step is a very short step. Next, he wants to walk into the defensive end and climb his frame (Diagram #3). We can drill the block with the entire group or we can run them one at a time and check each player on his technique. I always make sure I am watching one of the five groups. We always comment on one of the blockers all of the time. We just want to make sure no one is taking a play off.

Diagram #3. Base One-Man-Removed Block

If the blocker goes long with the second step, he cannot handle the spike or blitz they may bring. We open up with the near foot, gaining width and depth and going short with the second foot. When we work on this drill, remember we can go outside or we can go inside with the ball. The same blocking technique would apply to the play if you are going inside or outside on the play.

Let me make sure you understand what we are doing here. On these drills, every footwork technique that we use on the inside-zone play or the inside-gap play is going to be done in this five-minute pre-practice period. I know college and high school line coaches have a hard time finding time to work this into their individual period. You give them third-down situations and you give them all kinds of things that take up more and more of your time. This drill only takes us about five minutes.

Whatever we do in a drill as a technique, I want to see it replicated in the game film. Moreover, we all know it doesn't always show up in the game films. At times, when we go through our game films, I have a hard time finding plays where our players are doing what they are suppose to do.

Our next block is the base cutoff block. This is the backside block. We have more of a problem on the backside than we do on the frontside. This is particularly true on the inside runs. There are a lot of ways we block this play. We see teams that use the rip move, and we see some teams that try to jump hook our block.

I grew up on a farm. We would go out on the town on Saturday night. If we got the pickup truck stuck in the mud, we did not dare call our dads because they may smell the beer on our breath. So we would push the truck out of the mud. We would push the truck sideways with one person up front steering the truck. That usually worked for us. It was a good leverage tool and was effective for us.

On the cutoff block, we use the same leverage principle. This block is for the backside tackle or guard, and the play is going on the other side of the center. The first thing we do on the techniques is to "pick up and sit down." It is the same as we did in the drill earlier. As I bring the near foot through, I want to grab the outside part of the shoulder pad that fits over the heart. I want to grab the bottom part of that shoulder pad with my near hand. I do not hold the pad, I clutch the pad. If I hold onto the pad, it is holding, and they will call that in the NFL.

I want to get into the defender tight. Then, I take the outside hand and place it on the same part of the shoulder pad as I did on the opposite side. As I make contact on the near shoulder pad, I want to run my hips through the defender inside.

I am not trying to turn the defender. However, if I can get my hips even with his hips, I can turn him. If I cannot get him turned and he comes over my head, I take him the way he is going and push him down the line. I do not want him to push me back where my body ends up in the way of the play. If the defender comes inside, we want to take him off the line of scrimmage so he does not end up in the area where we are running the ball on the frontside.

We want to work the defenders on an angle off the line of scrimmage. If the defender lines up inside the blocker, it is just a greater angle on the block. The angle is determined by the distance the defender is to the blocker. If I am the tackle and the defender is in a 3 technique, the angle is a lot less. If he is already lined up inside, I may have to increase my angle.

If we can take the defender off the line of scrimmage, it gives us a better chance to make the cutback on the play. We want to turn our hips into the defender and take him off the line of scrimmage. When the running back does cut back, it gives him a little more room to run past the defenders.

On all of the individual base techniques, we are teaching fit into a combination block that we will cover later.

The next technique is for our blocker that is covered and he has a shade on the blocker. It is a technique used on the combination block. That means we are going to have help from someone on my team. This technique can be used on all of our combination blocks.

This is what we want. This could be our right guard on a deuce block. The outside blocker could be the tackle on the combination block. If the defender is in a 3 technique, I want vertical movement on the defender. The technique for the guard is this: The first step by the guard is a settle step with the far foot (Diagram #4). The second step goes up and into the defender. We make contact and we are the "lifter" in the double-team block.

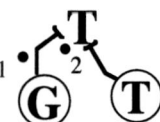

Diagram #4. Double-Team Block

We are trying to keep the leg away from the defender high. On the first move, we want that leg high. We want that first settle step high, and the second step with the near foot should be a short step. We want the first step into the ground and the second step up into the defender, and then we hit and lift. Remember the inside man is the lifter. We talk about the technique in that we *settle*, *hit*, and *lift*. We want the blocker's chest to be over his knee. We want that first man to hit and lift.

The second man is the "kill" man. We cannot get the lift if the pads of the first blocker are too high. He has to stay down low. We want the second step up and into the defender. It is a hit-and-lift movement.

The thing about the steps for the inside man is this: By taking the settle step and then the step to get up and into the defender, we have a chance to pick up the defender if he slants inside. The first step is a settle step, and the second step is to get the near foot up and into the defender. Again, the angle against the defender determines the type of block we are going to use. It may be a deuce block on the playside, or it may be a split block on the backside with the backside guard and tackle.

I want to stress we do all of these blocks in the first five minutes of practice. We do them every day. During the season, we do them all as a group. In the off-season we do them one man at a time.

Our next technique is the gallop block against an adjacent defender. This term comes from Jim McNally. About five or six years ago, I was coaching the Cleveland Browns. Jim was coaching with the New York Giants. He called me and asked me to look at the film of one of his plays. We had the system where we could get on the computers and view film from different teams. Jim told me to check out the blocking on a play to see if I thought it would work. It was an ace block, which was a double-team block with the center and right guard on the backside linebacker. He asked me to watch Ron Stone who was the right guard.

Jim asked me what I thought about the blocking. I told him that it was a good blocking scheme. I was really thinking, *you cannot do that*, but I did not want to hurt Jim's feelings about the play. I told Jimmy that the play looked good. Then, I started thinking about the play, and the more I thought

about it, it looked like a scheme that really would work.

What is the number-one thing you must have on the double-team block? It is this: Ass to ass. You cannot run a double-team block if there is daylight between the butts of the two blockers. They must fit their butts together just as you fit your knuckles together on the back of your hands. If they do not have their butts together, they are working against each other and nothing is happening.

The two blockers must end up together under the defender. They must drive the defender back and off the line of scrimmage. The question is how do we get to that point? The best way to get to that point is to line up toe to toe or just foot to foot. However, we do not want to do that. Here is the problem we always had on this block. As the tackle steps up on the block, his right foot is up and on the outside of the defender. Then, he brings up the inside foot, and it leaves a gap between the guard and tackle on the block.

To make the block more effective, we use some of the terminology that Jim McNally used. We called the *block* gallop to indicate how we are going to handle that situation. It may look a little goofy at first. Instead of taking the settle step, the level-off step, and a third step into the defender, we take the settle step, another settle step with that inside foot, and then we take the third step into the defender (Diagram #5). Now, we have established the high-leg technique. We want both blockers with the inside let up high on the play. This is a gallop technique. It is short step with the inside foot, another short step with the inside foot, and then the third step with the outside foot (Diagram #5). Now, we can align with our butt next to the inside blocker's butt.

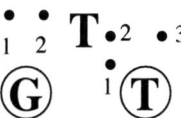

Diagram #5. Gallop-Block Technique

We can run the gallop techniques as a linemen working on the double-team block. We use this block on a shade technique.

I do not believe the two men on the double-team block must arrive at the point of contact against the defender at the same time. The set-up man or the man that is standing him up should be there first. The high man can come in second, crack the defender in the ribs, and drive him back off the line of scrimmage.

I do not care about the backside linebackers. The frontside worries about the linebacker coming through the A gap. The backside blocker worries about the linebacker as an afterthought. We want movement on the inside blocker. We want the gallop movement, and then we want to climb block on the defender. Again, we want the blockers to keep the inside leg high. You must be able to cover some ground when you use the gallop block. We do not want the blocker to step back on the play. The second short step looks a little different, but it allows him to get the position on the defender he needs to make the double-team.

Sometimes, we have a double-team block against a defender that does not leave us anything to double-team. That could be a defender playing a 0 technique. I do not know if many of you are seeing the 4-3 defense today, but we are playing against a lot of 4-3 teams. The defense plays a 0 technique on the alignment. On occasion, we get teams that play a head-up technique against our guard. We want to double-team the 0 technique or the 2 technique on the guard, but the defenders are not leaving you anything to hit. We double-team the defender on the outside shoulder of the offensive linemen. Now, the defender is head-up and does not give us a blocking target.

Let me give you the situation. We have a nose man over the center. I am the right guard and we are going to double-team the nose man back to the backside linebacker. The nose does not leave much of his body to aim for on the double-team from the side where the guard is coming from. We see blockers that get their shoulders turned toward the

sideline and do not get their butts inside to the center. They do not get anything done. They end up in a bad position to block the scrape linebacker. When that happens, we do not have a double-team block. We do not have anything when that happens. We end up wasting a player on that block.

Here is the thing you should remember. If you are looking at a tape or film on zone-type plays, gap-type plays, and lead plays, if you cannot see both numbers on the backs of the jerseys of the two blockers, then something is wrong. When I am looking at our tapes and I cannot see the blocker's numbers on the back of his jersey, I know we have a problem.

We are going to use the gallop block again in that situation. Before, when we had a 3 technique, we used the gallop block on a lateral step. Now that I face a 0 technique, I am going to gallop step off the line of scrimmage, toward the defender. I do not want to step inside and get all tangled up with the center. We gallop up with the inside foot, take another gallop step with the inside foot, and then step with the outside foot toward the defender, keeping our butts inside and parallel to the line of scrimmage. Now, we want to try to hit the defender in the ribs (Diagram #6). We do not want to push him or get our hands on his. If we do that, we get our numbers turned. I will guarantee you they do not like that hit to the ribs. This will allow our outside blocker to make the play, and then get to the backside linebacker.

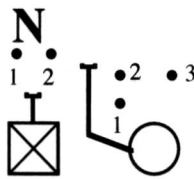

Diagram #6. Gallop vs. Adjacent 0 Technique

Because the noseguards are so smart, we do not take the step with the far foot. If we do that, the noseguard knows we are going to double-team him. He knows the step with the far foot is made to give the right guard additional room for the double-team. When he sees that move, he splits the block between the center and the guard. Now, we have the center explode into the nose man to keep him from splitting the block. We do not want the center to step away because the nose will split the gap when he sees that move.

If we can do the individual drills and work on them for five minutes each day, we get the footwork included in the blocks.

The San Diego Chargers play the double-team block as well as anyone. When we get into the games, I tell our players I do not want you to be thinking about your techniques when you come off the ball—I want you to think about mauling somebody. I tell the players if they do their techniques correctly in practice, then they can go out in the games and get after people.

I tell the players to watch the martial arts experts. When those guys go to the ground, it is all technique. They are bad dudes and they are strong, but they get after it. However, it is still technique. It is the same in football. When you get into the trenches in football, it is like mixed-martial-arts guys on the ground. It is a matter of technique. It is the same as playing football.

Just remember the fact that we want our double-team players with their butts side by side so we can see the numbers on the backs of their jerseys. That is a simple rule, but it works very well. We do not want the defender to split us on the double-team block.

The question has come up about the 3 technique that is in a tilt stance. He lines up with his shoulders turned inside toward the center. We do not change our technique when we see that man in a tilt alignment. If he is in a shade technique, we block it the same as if he were in a normal stance with his shoulders square to the line of scrimmage. The one thing I would be concerned about on the tilt is where we make contact with the defender. We would prefer to hit him on the hip as opposed to his shoulder. We have always tried to hit the man in the ribs and lift him out of the hole. Some of the things that we do that need to be consistent on these types of blocks include the different alignments we face, such as the tilted defensive linemen.

The double-team block with the center and guard is the ace block. Next, I want to talk about the playside guard and the playside tackle on the double-team block on to the linebacker. We use this on lead plays. The drills we showed you earlier are rapid-fire type blocks. We do those drills early in practice. Now, we are taking the deuce block. If we are blocking against the shade on the double-team, the outside man can gallop and get into the block without a lot of effort. If the defender is in a 0 technique, the outside man must gallop step and get upfield so he is even with the center. He has to make sure he gets his shoulders square and gets upfield to make the double-team block effective. We would prefer for the center to explode on the nose man. He must do enough footwork to keep his momentum going.

The center is not using his flipper on the block. He is using his hands. The only flipper we get out of the gallop man is when he bangs the defender in the ribs on the double-team.

We do not want the center to get up on his toes when he is blocking a 0 technique. When he gets up on his toes, he is not going to win that battle. We want him to stay square on the man with his weight on the balls of his feet. He must stay under control and keep his pads square. We do not want him up on his toes.

Next is the backside guard/center double-team block to the linebacker. Again, we use this technique on lead plays (Diagram #7). All of the techniques we use here have been done in drills earlier in practice. We can get movement if we can get butt to butt on the technique.

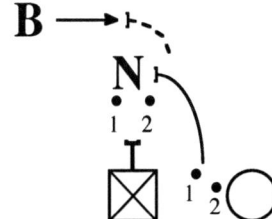

Diagram #7. Guard/Center Double-Team Block/Linebacker

The next block we see is the playside strong tackle/tight end double-team block to the linebacker. We use this technique on lead plays. The tackle and tight end do the same type of block that the other linemen use.

Next is the block on the uncovered zone defender (Diagram #8). Our technique on the uncovered zone block is big in our offense. I think you can get in too big of a hurry on this block to get to the second level. We are talking about the alignment if I am a right guard and I am uncovered, and the right tackle is covered, and the center is covered. I do not need to be in a hurry to get up into the second level. If I get up in the line too quickly, it means I have to hold the block a longer time. We do not want to leave the first level too fast.

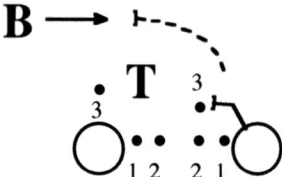

Diagram #8. Uncovered Lineman Block

Our technique is to help our adjacent lineman and to get up on the upper linebacker. We take three steps before we make contact. We step with the near foot on a short step, then we take another lateral step with the near foot, and then we come up on the block with the third step (Diagram #9). It is boom, boom, and then boom. That second step is a lateral step, but it is a short step. You do not have to be in a hurry to get to that second level.

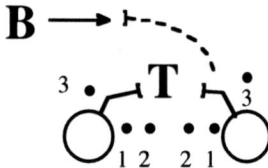

Diagram #9. Uncovered Lineman/Linebacker

In practice, working on the uncovered zone, we work on the right side first, and then we go to the left side. That only takes about five seconds.

The technique on the inside-zone play is different from what we use on this block. If you play against a team that uses a 0 technique, you must use a different block in that situation. The center must stay with the nose man longer. He should darn near base block that 0 technique. We want the center to put his face slightly to the playside. Just put the face slightly to the playside and base block the play. The defense is looking for the center to put his face to the playside so they can fall off to the backside. The center must put his face to the playside and then drive him like he does on a base block to keep him from sliding to the backside. The center must do what he needs to do against the type of players he is playing against. He can make the block for the guard a lot easier if he can drive that nose man off the line.

Let me talk about the playside guard and center zone block to the linebacker. We use this on the inside-zone plays. We do the same thing with the center on the play (Diagram #10). We call this a single block. The center sees the 3 techniques outside on the guard. The center laterally gallops toward the 3 technique in case he slants inside. He is there to pick him up. If the 3 technique stretches, he has his shoulder pads square to block the linebacker. This is a single block to us.

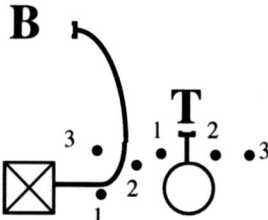

Diagram #10. Single Block, Center/Guard

A single block to use is anytime the center and right guard are working against the right tackle and linebacker. We make sure we know the technique we are using. This is an example of an uncovered technique for the center and a zone technique for the right guard (Diagram #11).

The next technique we are looking at is the settle step move on a 3 technique and a Mike linebacker. We teach the guard to take a settle step

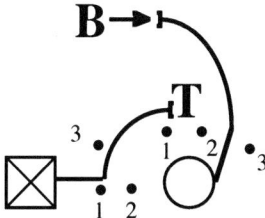

Diagram #11. Single Block, Guard/Center

and to get the second step up into the defender, hit, lift and ricochet to the Mike linebacker. I am trying to evaluate this block because of what we are seeing now on this block. This is what we are seeing. All bubble linebackers on the inside-zone plays are looking, looking, and then folding over to the backside. Depending on the opponent, we may have to stay on the block a little longer.

Let me show you the same blocks with the center and the guard against the 3 technique and the linebacker. First, we have the center taking the 3 technique and the guard picking up the linebacker (Diagram #12). Both linemen use the techniques that have been taught repeatedly. The near man takes that short step and a second short step, and then he takes the near foot and brings the knee up high into the defender. He takes the defender on the line of scrimmage. The linebacker comes off for the linebacker.

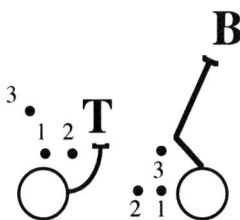

Diagram #12. Center Blocks 3 Technique/Guard Blocks Linebacker

The other part of the block is just the opposite (Diagram #13). If that linebacker is anxious to fold over the top to get to the backside, the center can pick him up and the guard takes the 3 technique, which is the down lineman.

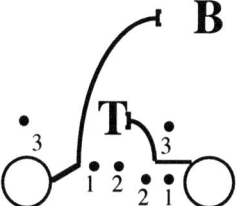

Diagram #13. Center Blocks Linebacker/Guard Blocks Down 3 Technique

I am rethinking the technique because we are seeing so many of the linebackers folding over to the backside. Depending on our opponent, we are going to stay on the blocks a little longer until we figure out what we want to do on the play.

Next, I want to look at the under defense. We have a shade on the center and a man outside of the tackle (Diagram #14).

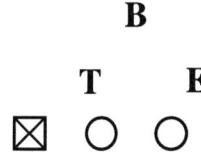

Diagram #14. Shade on Center

We are either going to double, which means the center and right guard, or we are going to single block. The guard makes the call. He just calls out *single* or *double*.

We do this so we all know what we are doing. If it is a single block, the guard gets the second step up into the defender and moves to the linebacker (Diagram #16). The center single blocks the shade defender.

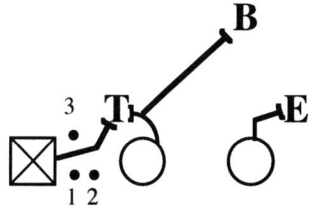

Diagram #15. Single Block

The technique for the guard on the play is this: The near foot goes up and down in place. The next foot is to hit and push off the other foot upfield. If I am the right guard, I want to lift the near foot and sit it down, take a step up toward the down lineman with the opposite foot, and then take another step with that opposite foot and push off and step into the man with the near foot. If you only take a short step with the near foot and then take only one step with the opposite foot and then step into the man, you are off balance. If you do that, it forces you to take an additional step to get your balance, and you cannot make contact if you are off balance. It is boom, boom, boom, and then step up with the near foot to make contact with the linebacker.

Our next block is the backside guard and center on a zone block that we use on the inside-zone plays. This is a center and a backside guard move. All of the individual blocks we have talked about earlier are made on the combination blocks. Even if we do not have time to work on the scoop block during the week, we at least have worked the component parts of the block.

I want to make one coaching point on the scoop play. It is difficult to break the habit of trying to reach block the down lineman after you have used the reach block for so many years. We want the center to push the defender to the strongside, and we are going to push the ball to the backside. We want to keep our base block and force the defender to play the ball to the strongside, and we want the back to cut the ball back into the hole on the backside.

We do not want the offensive left guard going for the linebacker too quickly. It is a constant battle to keep him from flying toward that linebacker. He must not rush the play. If he will take those two steps toward the down lineman and then make that third step, he has a chance to come off and get the linebacker. We want to get all of our techniques down where we can count on them in all situations. We see some good techniques—we just do not see them all at one time enough.

The last block is the backside guard and the backside tackle on the zone block to the linebacker. Again, we use this combination on the inside-zone

plays. Once you have done one technique, you are doing all of the techniques. It is just a matter of your angles may be changing. This is the slip block (Diagram #16). The same techniques are being used. I am sure it is getting to be repetitive. All of the techniques we did before are now being used in the team drills.

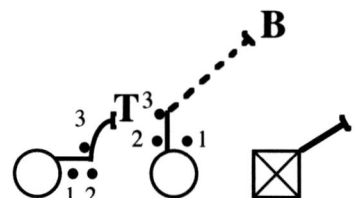

Diagram #16. Slip Block

The last point here is on the down-the-line drill. All we are doing here is working on the backside cutoff block. The angle on the pull is vital. This block is used to cut a man on the wide play. We take the front five linemen and we have the backside guard and tackle place their toe on the line. Then, we tell them to turn and run but do not cross the line to their left side. We want them to open up the hips and run (Diagram #17). By running this drill, the players get the feel for where they can make the backside cutoff block. We are not an outside-zone play team, and it is not something that we are great at doing. We line up two groups and run one group, and then we run the other group. If they cross the line, it means they have run into the defender they are supposed to be cutting. We want them to pull, turn, and run, and then cut.

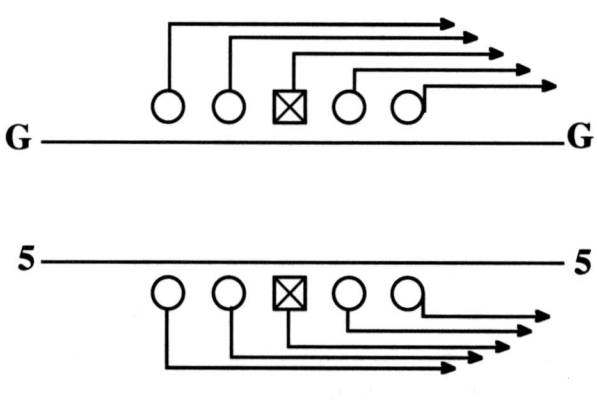

Diagram #17. Pull, Turn, and Run

If I am the right guard pulling to the left, I want to put my toe on the line. Then, I pull going left, and I do not cross the white line. We are working on that angle.

Now, I want to talk about the Steelers' draw play. Let me give you some background on the play. John Masco was the line coach of the New Orleans Saints and he was studying this play. I asked him to make me a copy of the study. He sent me a copy and I studied the tape. It is a little different type of draw play, and I do not see a lot of people running the play the way he did. We run the play, and Indianapolis has run the same play forever. Howard Mudd and Tom Moore have been at Indianapolis a long time, and they have run the play for 11 years.

The reason this play is called the Steelers' draw is because Tom Moore was at Pittsburgh in the early 1990s and they ran this draw play. The tape that John Masco had is the tape I learned the play from and included it in our system. We ran it when I coached at Tulane University and when I was at the University of Cincinnati. We did not run the play when I coached at Cleveland or Buffalo. We are running the play now with the Pittsburgh Steelers.

First, I am going to show you the play, and then I am going to talk with you about the play later. We just call the play the Steelers' draw. I think you can look at this play as if it were a delayed outside zone play. Also, it is similar to a screen pass as I watch Tom Lovat run the screen pass. It is like a delayed outside-zone play, and the linebackers are hanging inside as if they are expecting the outside-zone play.

I do want to tell you two very important points on the draw play. The ball needs to be handed off at five and a half yards deep in the backfield. It can be handed off at six yards and still work. The left tackle that is going to do double duty, his outside foot needs to hit back at three and a half yards on his drop. You may say that is too much and that you have trouble getting your linemen to drop that deep. Yes, you can! It is set until they figure out where the point is at three and a half yards deep.

Here is the theory of the play. The onside tackle is going to do double duty on the play. Against a 3x1

alignment, he is going to check for the corner blitz and then go downfield and block a secondary defender. The back is going to get the handoff five and a half yards deep. As soon as he clears the defensive end, he is going to cut outside toward the sideline. Now, what we have is the stretch play outside. However, we get to that point by running the draw play.

I know a lot of you are running the spread offense now. You have three wide and you have four wide. You can run this play out of formation. You can run it out of a 3x1, a 2x2, a 4 wide, and you can run it out of two tight ends.

I want to go over the concepts of the plays and cover the key coaching points. First, I want to show you the play in a 2x2 alignment, and in a 3x1 alignment. I am going to use a standard 4-2 defense in both plays.

The question is who to block. We are going to declare the Mike linebacker. Then, all of our rules come off him. One point you need to know. It is not the true Mike. It could be another linebacker to us. For us, it is one player that we determine as our Mike defender.

We are facing six in the box. We are going to declare the playside inside backer as our Mike (Diagram #18). Then, our rules come off this principle. I could go into additional ways in determining who the Mike is against the three-man line, but I want you to get this principle down first. Our rules come off the man we determine as the Mike.

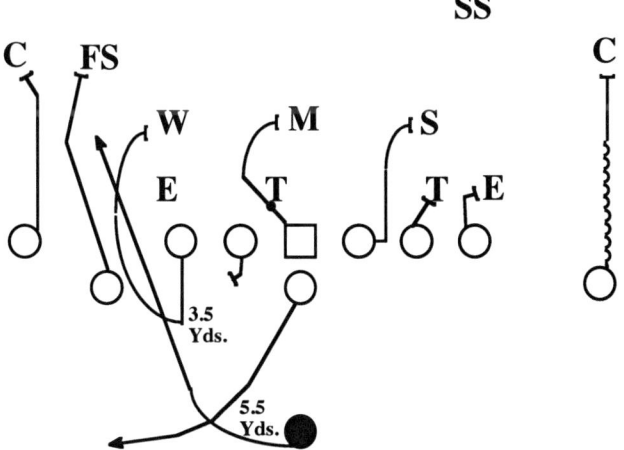

Diagram #18. 2x2 Alignment

Our left tackle, or playside tackle in this case, is going to set with his outside foot hitting the ground at three and a half yards back and outside. Then, he is going to go on a flat angle outside as if he were blocking the stretch play; he would be able to block the slot defender in this case. The slot receiver should bypass the slot defender and head downfield toward the safety. The split end goes for the corner on his side.

If you are going to run these plays, make sure you adhere to these points. The ball must be handed off at five and a half yards to six yards deep. The playside tackle's outside foot must hit at three-and-a-half yards deep. We used to say the tackle should drop back four yards, but, for some reason, three and a half yards works better now.

What we do with the onside guard is similar to the slide protection. He slides, but he also gets some depth. If the defensive tackle wants to come upfield, we want the guard to get a hand on him as he slides to the outside. He is not going to make the play going inside because the ball is going outside. If we happen to get a dog blitz by Mike, the guard is there to pick him up. If the end slants down inside, the guard is there to pick him up. We want the onside guard to drop to his outside with three short steps. He does not need to worry about where the defense is coming from. We want him to get to his spot. If the end comes inside on an E-T stunt, the guard blocks the end. If the shade 2i comes upfield, we want the guard to get a hand on him and make sure he goes inside. He is not going to make the play.

The center comes flat off the line and tries to hook the Mike backer. The backside guard and tackle run a power slip on the tackle and linebacker. The end blocks the defensive end.

Now, we look at the 3x1 alignment. There has been a lot of thought into this play. Before we used to declare the Mike inside if the defense had a free safety in the middle of the field. The onside tackle had to drop step, and then go back up inside to pick up the Will backer that lined up inside in a stack behind the defensive tackle. It was never a good deal for us.

The other thing is the fact that we started to see more split defenses on third down. When the Mike was declared, we still had to take our onside tackle to go back inside on the Will backer. In our experiences, it was not good when our tackle had to go back inside to block on the backer.

What we decided to do was to declare the playside linebacker our Mike when we were in a 1x3 formation. The onside tackle takes his three-and-a-half drop and looks for the corner blitz. If the corner is not coming, he goes downfield to pick up the free safety or the Will backer if he is chasing him (Diagram #19). The other players run their normal assignments.

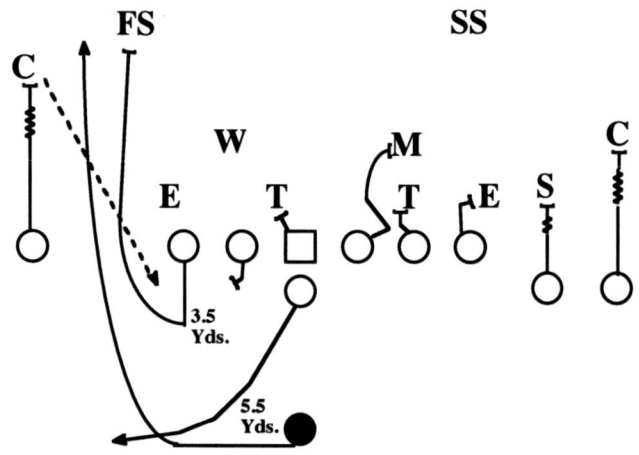

Diagram #19. 1x3 Alignment

It is an interesting play in that you can handle twist plays, you can handle blitz moves and just about anything the defense throws at you.

We have a tendency to check out of the play when we see a blitz coming. I would really like to run it into a blitz. It is a feast or famine type of play. The play ends up as a 15- to 20-yard gain or a six-yard loss. That is the type of play it is been for us. Halfway through the season, it was averaging 13 yards per carry for us. It ended up around 10 yards per play for us.

At one time, this is what we did against six-in-the-box type defense. If the Will and defensive end both came on a blitz, we had the tackle drop three yards and block the Will coming inside (Diagram #20).

We blocked the inside man and let the outside man go. If he ran up the field, he ended up too deep and the back ran past him. As I said, it was either feast or famine.

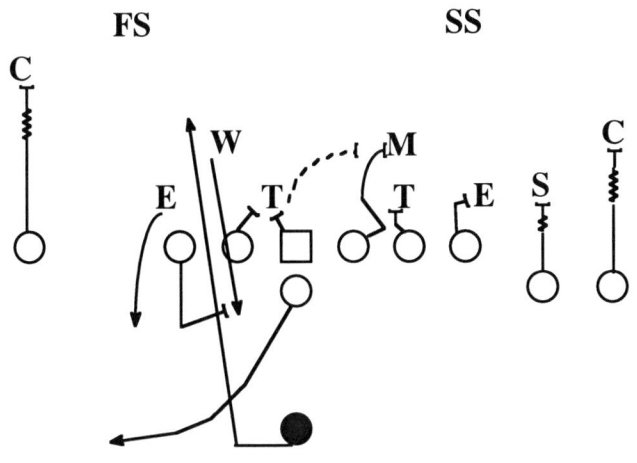

Diagram #20. Tackle Block on Will

Because we put the tag on the end of the play, we got scared out of running the play against the blitz.

Let me show you want I love to see out of the 2x2 alignment. I love to see the defense bring the Will backer off the corner (Diagram #21). You will see on tape that Will is not going to make the play.

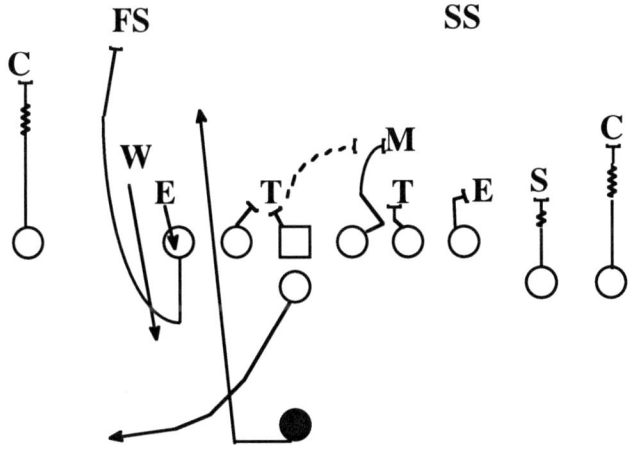

Diagram #21. Vs. Will Blitz

It is not as good against the corner blitz (Diagram #22). Because of the distance, the corner has time to adjust on the play. He can adjust and tackle the running back. The Will does not have time to adjust on the play.

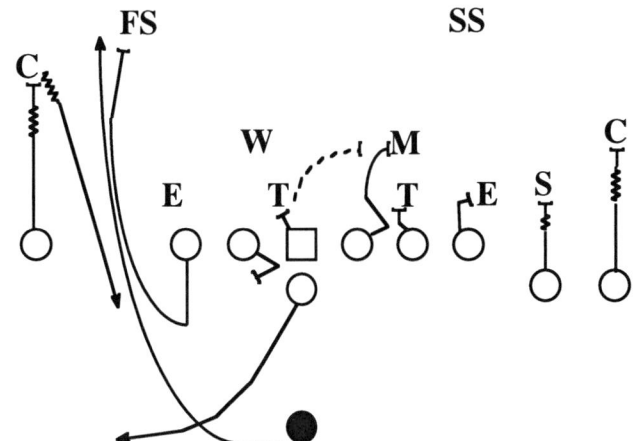

Diagram #22. Corner Blitz

Next, I want to put on a tape to show you the Steelers' draw play. I will try to coach it as we go through the film. If the handoff is too deep, the end can make the play. If the handoff is too shallow, the end will make the tackle. It has to be in the correct spot to be successful.

If the onside tackle drops too deep on his first step, you are out of sync. If he steps too short, you are out of sync.

We want the center to be flat on the play. One good thing about running the draw outside on the edge is that we get away from a lot of traffic inside. Another thing about running the draw is the fact that, at times, the linebackers go unblocked but they still do not make the play. It is because they cannot overcome the inertia. They are sitting on ready and they are on the edge of their toes waiting to go. They know it is a draw, but they just cannot get to the play in time.

When we face a seven-man front, as a rule, we declare the first linebacker, and double duty to the second linebacker. One point that Tom Lovat made this morning is important. When we get outside, we want to make the defense come to us on the blocking on this play.

One point I do want to make is with the playside tackle. We do not want him to overset. What I mean by overset is that we do not want to take a long, exaggerated step and have the defender come inside and beat the blocker. However, on this draw, you want to overstep to encourage the defender to go inside. What we want is for the ball to get outside, and the sooner it gets outside, the better off we are. If the defensive end comes inside, we tell the back to get going and get outside of the defensive end. The play does not have to be blocked perfectly to gain some big yards.

If we run the play out of the shotgun formation, we have to make an adjustment. The back is in his normal stance. The tackle makes the adjustment by taking a three-foot drop instead of the three and a half. That makes the timing a lot better on the play. The players know how deep they need to drop on the plays. The players are very good at adapting to the different formations.

We hate to run this play into a 3 technique. Running into a 3 technique can be real bad business. We try to overset him to make him feel that he can beat us inside. Then, if the guard gets the inside hand on the 3 technique, he is out of the play as he comes inside.

That is the end of the tape and the lecture. That is it. Have a good season next year. Thank you.

ABOUT THE AUTHOR

Larry Zierlein completed his second season coaching the Steelers' offensive line with a Super Bowl win. Zierlein was hired on January 29, 2007, by first-year head coach Mike Tomlin.

Zierlein, 62, went to Pittsburgh after previously serving as the assistant offensive line coach for the Buffalo Bills. Prior to his one-year stint in Buffalo, Zierlein was the offensive line coach for the Cleveland Browns for four seasons (2001 to 2004). His work with Cleveland's offensive line helped the Browns average 4.1 yards per rush and 104.4 rushing yards per game in 2003.

Zierlein, who has 38 years of coaching experience, spent the previous four seasons before joining the Browns as offensive line coach for the University of Cincinnati (1997 to 2000). During the 2000 season, Zierlein also served as the Bearcats' running game coordinator and helped Cincinnati set a Conference USA rushing record with 215.5 yards per game in 1997. From that line, tackle Jason Fabini was a fourth-round draft choice of the New York Jets. Zierlein's 1999 line led the nation by allowing a school-record low eight sacks, despite having four first-year starters.

Prior to his tenure at Cincinnati, Zierlein spent two seasons at Tulane (1995 to 1996) and Louisiana State (1993 to 1994). He also served as offensive line coach at the University of Houston (1978 to 1986).

Zierlein gained experience at the professional level as co-offensive coordinator and offensive line coach for the New York/New Jersey Knights of the World League of American Football (WLAF) in 1991 to 1992 and as an assistant coach for the Washington Commandos of the Arena Football League in 1987.

In addition to coaching, Zierlein also served in the United States Marine Corps for two years (1966 to 1968), including a one-year tour of duty in Vietnam (1967).

A 1971 graduate of Fort Hays Kansas State College, Zierlein began his coaching career at Fort Hays State College as linebackers coach in 1970. After two years at Fort Hays State, he spent six years at the high school level, coaching at Abernathy (Texas) High School from 1972 to 1974 and Lamar Consolidated (Texas) High School from 1975 to 1977

A native of Lenora, Kansas, Zierlein and his wife, Marcia, have three children, sons Lance and Mike, and daughter Nicci, and grandchildren Alec, Drake, Ellie, Maggie, and Mason.

ZIERLEIN AT A GLANCE

- 2007-present: Pittsburgh Steelers, Offensive Line Coach
- 2006: Buffalo Bills, Offensive Line Coach
- 2001-2004: Cleveland Browns, Offensive Line Coach
- 1997-2000: University of Cincinnati, Offensive Line Coach
- 1995-1996: Tulane University, Offensive Line Coach
- 1993-1994: Louisiana State University, Offensive Line Coach
- 1991-1992: New York/New Jersey Knights, Offensive Line Coach
- 1987: Washington (AFL), Offensive Line Coach
- 1978-1986: University of Houston, Offensive Line Coach

PAUL ALEXANDER, TOM BRATTAN, MIKE FOLEY, STACY SEARELS

Question-and-Answer Session

Paul Alexander (moderator): At this time, we are going to our question-and-answer session. We will address the questions to the college speakers, but we will not eliminate the pro speakers that are here as well.

Question: What is the difference in the press steps on the quick game, as compared to the five- or seven-step drops?

Stacy Searels: In our quick game, we are going to try to get their hands down and we are going to cut them. We do some drills where I set the backs up to the outside of the leftside blockers. We take a quick set and we throw at the bare legs. That is how we teach the quick pass. If the defender is rushing upfield, the far leg is going to be his outside leg. If he comes inside on the rush, his bare leg is the inside leg. That is for our quick set.

On a five-step or seven-step drop, if the blocker is in the full slide, we will be man protection and slide inside. On the other side, we are sorting in our gaps. We have A gap, B gap, and C gap. We do not want the inside foot coming outside. It is the same as we taught on the board drill. We do not teach our lineman to go straight back on the drop. If the blocker is on the slide side, he can sit outside a little more. It changes if you are slide blocking or blocking on the near defender. It changes based on what the defense is doing.

Paul Alexander: Here is a perspective on the quick game. When I joined the Bengals 16 years ago, Jim McNally was the line coach. Of course, I was always asking the questions. I was coaching the tight ends. The question that always blew my mind was this: On a three-step drop, what do you do on the man side when they run the twist? If you set too short

and they twist, you are dead. If you set too far back, the defense will push you back. So the question is what to do on the man side when they run the twist? Here is the answer Jim gave me. He said, "I look at the script, and I tell them in the huddle before the play to watch for the twist. That kept me thinking, why make it miserable on Wednesday when we know it is going to be miserable on Sunday."

Question: The line is running the kick-out block with the wingback going back and forth on the goal line, how do you change up those blocks?

Tom Brattan: We are working on the outside with the wingback kicking out the first man on the outside leg of the tackle. We play it several ways. If the Sam linebacker is wide, we can swap the block and have the wingback block the end, and the tight end can block the Sam backer.

Paul Alexander: We have run that play before. It has never been real good for us. We ran it with an isolation action, and that is why it did not work. We did not take advantage of that kick-out block. We are going to change the path of the back on that play to take advantage of the kick-out block.

Question: If you face seven in the box and you are in a one-back set and you have a power play called, what do you do?

Tom Brattan: If we face seven in the box, some of the decisions we make depend on what they align against our formation. If we face an under front, we would check out of the play. If we face a pro front or a 4-3 look, and if the Will linebacker is on the backside of the play, we would put the tackle in cutoff and climb block so we could try to block two men with one blocker on that play on the backside.

Most of the time, we see a basic 4-2 nickel defense, which is basic. The teams rotate the linebackers over to make it look like a 4-3 pro look. They try to cheat the Will backer inside. We try to combat this by cutting off the backside tackle, and climbing the Will linebacker.

Question: Where do you want the blocker to aim his eyes in a fundamental 1-on-1 block?

Stacy Searals: Good question. What I talked about was the 1-on-1 block. In the film, we had a player that punched with his inside hand to the defender's nearest shoulder pad. We want our blocker to look at the tip of the shoulder pad.

If we are in slide protection, where we are soaring to one side, and we see a linebacker between the center and guard, that is not the guard's responsibility. If he is the left guard and he has a 2i defender on him, that is his man. You do not have to look at the linebacker. If the linebacker comes on a blitz, we have a problem. We have a body presence with the 2i. If the 2i does not come, we look inside to the gap. That is the way we block the 1-on-1 or if the man is in the slot as to where we want to aim our eyes.

For the guards, if we are in man protection, we want to get on the defender as quickly as possible. We want to jump on him right now. We teach it sort of like we teach run blocking. We teach the theory that the wider the defender, the deeper we will go on. It's the same as we teach on the zone play. The tighter the defender is, the tighter our feet are to the line of scrimmage. If he is tight on the line, the quicker we want to get on the defender. It is according to what their alignment is.

Paul Alexander: I want to introduce one of our Bengal players to illustrate a point. Come up here, Andrew Whitworth. He is our left tackle and he is one hell of a player. I want him to show you how he sets his hands on a power set. [Editor's Note: Andrew demonstrates setting the hands on a power set.] Now, who has a question for Andrew?

He is going to become a great football coach. He really understands football.

Question: What skills do you use on the power play?

Andrew Whitworth: We talk about taking smart splits. If we are in combination blocks and we are using the trade blocks, we want to cut the split down to one and a half to two feet. It could be the tight end and tackle working together, or it could be the guard and tackle working together; they are the ones that will cut the split down. If the defense is in an under look on the frontside, the tackle and tight end may have a foot-and-a-half split. The tackle can take a two–foot to a two-and-a-half-yard split from the guard. The guard will cut his split down from the center because he is going to be working on the nose technique.

For the backside guard, I want a two-foot split minimum for the pull. If he gets too tight, he gets to the point of attack too fast and we do not get much out of our guard. We split the backside tackle with a two-and-a-half- to a three-foot split.

Question: How do you teach the guard to pull when he is in a four-point stance when you are down on the goal line?

Tom Brattan: Sometimes we have the pulling guard in a 3-point stance. The line comes up, and in a short period, the snap is made. If the defense can read the guard in the 3-point stance that quickly, we are taking too long on the snap count.

We may have the guard back off the line a few inches. It is something we work on in pre-practice. We come out and work on those bird-dog drills and the wing-T drills. We go from a 4-point stance and take our steps. You must work on the steps in practice. We do our cutoff blocks the same way.

On the pull, I am going to put my weight on my backside foot, and I drop my inside foot, and pull. I have done skip-pull and the drop-step. We do not skip-pull by nature. Asking the players to learn another block on the goal line is asking them to do one more thing, and they have enough to do now.

However, usually, you have weight on the back foot, you drop the playside foot, and you key the block on the way as you pull.

Paul Alexander: I think there are two schools of thought on the power play on how you pull. First is a power play that is real tight inside and up the middle. It is the A gap a lot of the times. On the power play, we pull the guard and kick out at the point of attack. They can trade blocks with the tight end or the lead back. When we pull on that type of play, we want the shoulders squared. Sometimes, you use a skip-pull as Ohio State does.

The other type of power play is where the back runs a local route. We teach the back to read the block of the fullback on the kick-out. When we use that type of block, we use the open pull.

Question: How do you block the power play if the tackle is covered?

Mike Foley: The guard will be going down inside. The tackle and tight end will combo block on the tackle. It is the deuce to the trey block because the tackle is covered. It is a combo block with the tackle and end working together. It is no different from when the tackle has already slanted inside. If I am the tackle, I want to take my tight leverage move. If the hip of the defensive tackle is still in the hole as the end comes down, he will push it. If the hip is gone, he will go for the linebacker. It is no different than the defensive tackle lining up in the 5 and he slants down to the 4i. The end will look for the hips of the tackle and read the block. If the hip is gone, he looks for the linebacker.

Question: What are the things you look for in the film study against the defensive end on his pass rush?

Mike Foley: The first thing I am going to look for is to see which hand he has down on the ground. This is going to determine everything for us. We talked about the spot drill and getting his alignment between the blocker and the quarterback. The steps of the defender will determine the speed I am going to kick block. If it is a player that has his close

hand down to the blocker, which would be his left hand if he is on our left side. If that is the case, when he gets to the blocker, his attack mode is going to be on his third step. He steps one, two, three, and that is where he is going to make his decision to come. He is coming inside or outside when he makes his decision.

If this is a man with his right hand down, his steps are going to come later. They do not have to apologize, but they do not have as much speed. Their move comes later, and the power comes when they are ready to open up. When they open up, they get overpowered into the quarterback.

Next, I look for his habits. After he takes that third step, what is the first thing that he wants to do? We are all habitual creatures. We all have habits. I am going to look to see what his habits are. We want to know where his hands are when he makes that third step. Where does he carry his hands, and what does he do with them as he makes that third step? Does he like to cork a little when he is in his stance?

Then, we want to know what he is going to do if the tackle sets him inside. What does he like to do? If our tackle oversets him, what does he like to do? If you can, find his favorite moves and the things he does. What does he do when our tackle sets him either inside or outside? What are his answers to those two things. When I find out those things, then I can find a way to block him.

Question: What do you do if the strong safety is trapping and comes up the gap on a goal-line play?

Tom Brattan: We are only going to block on one level on the block at the point of attack. That is the way it is at the goal line. If the strong safety shows first, we will take him. If not, we will block the next man to show. If the strong safety shows first, we will take him. If we do not hit the hole just right, we will block the next man. If we face a balanced front, we have a field day because we have the numbers in that situation. We can line up in two wings, one back, and the defense does not know where to declare the adjuster to the middle of the field. We have the wings on the playside to block down on the play. It is another way to pick up another blocker.

Question: What is the step for the tight end on the 5-technique tackle?

Tom Brattan: The first step for the tight end against the 5 technique is this: His first step is a lateral step, and then he is going to work to the hip to where the tackle is sitting. When we work the guard and tackle on a deuce block, they take lateral steps. The tackle is going to work the inside number. They are trying to get a vertical push. The tackle and end on the trey block want to get vertical, but they also want to get some horizontal movement as well. We want them to open up that hole for us.

Question: Does the center block back on the 2i shade?

Mike Foley: A shade is different from a 2i. If we shade to the side of the power play, the guard takes his near foot and he wants to stick his nose in his armpit. In our power play, the guard knows if the nose crosses his face, the guard is responsible for the A gap. Therefore, he knows he has help on the frontside. We tell the guard to take his inside part of his outside or backside foot, and to step on the inside foot of the defender's inside foot.

If it is a tri-block, it comes down to who you are playing against. That comes from film study and other techniques we can pick up from the film. We want to know if they are penetrators or not. If they always penetrate, we are going to get in a 90-degree angle and come down after him. If it is against a defender that plays soft, we start more on the man to the middle or go for a 45-degree angle on the defender. It all depends on the film study and if you are in the game. We do run the play a lot, so we do get a chance to see how the defense is going to play against us.

Let's give the speakers a big hand. Thank you for doing a great job. It is now time for the pizza.

Bob Wylie joins the Saskatchewan Roughriders after spending the past two years as the offensive line coach in Winnipeg. The Blue Bombers' offensive line gave up the fewest number of quarterback sacks in the CFL during those seasons.

In Wylie's first year with Winnipeg, the Bomber hogs led the CFL in fewest quarterback sacks given up (27), despite the absence of centre Obby Khan for most of the year due to injury. That protection allowed quarterback Kevin Glenn to have the best season of his CFL career, passing for a league-best 5,114 yards. The Winnipeg offensive line also helped pave the way for running back Charles Roberts to rush for 1,379 yards (5.3 yards per carry), the second best individual total in the CFL in 2007, despite Roberts missing the final two regular season games due to injury.

Wylie holds a wealth of coaching experience from the collegiate and NFL ranks. He coached NFL Hall of Famer Anthony Muñoz during his last year at Tampa Bay and has coached seven Pro Bowlers and four Pro-Bowl alternates. Wylie owns a resume that boasts the unique distinction of having coached at five different levels of football: Pop Warner, junior high school, high school, college, and pro.

In 2004, Wylie coached the offensive line for the Arizona Cardinals. He coached the offensive line with the Chicago Bears from 1999 to 2003. Wylie's 2001 Bears offensive line led the league in fewest quarterback sacks allowed, surrendering a league low 17—more than 21 below the NFL average and 17 fewer than the team allowed in 2000. His offensive line paved the way for running back Anthony Thomas to be named NFL Offensive Rookie of the Year, the first Chicago running back to achieve the honor since Gale Sayers in 1965. Thomas's 1,000 yards rushing season marked the seventh time an offensive line under the direction of Wylie has provided a 1,000-yard rusher. Under his tutelage, Olin Kreutz developed into one of the top centers in the NFL as a six-time Pro Bowl selection (2001 to 2006) and a first-team All-Pro (2006). He also coached another Chicago Pro Bowler in tackle James "Big Cat" Williams.

From 1997 to 1998, Wylie was the tight ends coach for the Cincinnati Bengals. Bengals' running back Corey Dillon rushed for more than 1,000 yards in each of those seasons.

In 1996, Wylie served as the offensive line coach for the University of Cincinnati when the team led Conference USA in rushing (181.4 yards per game) as four Bearcat linemen earned post-season honors, including tackle Jason Fabini who has played for the New York Jets and the Dallas Cowboys.

Prior to working as the offensive line coach at the University of Cincinnati (1996), Wylie spent four seasons as the offensive line coach of the NFL's Tampa Bay Buccaneers (1992 to 1995). Wylie's line helped pave the way for running back Errict Rhett to rush for back-to-back 1,000-yard seasons his first two years in the league. At the time, Rhett was one of only five NFL running backs to accomplish that feat.

Wylie began his NFL coaching career in 1990 with the New York Jets. Serving as the tight ends coach and assisting the offensive line coach, he spent two seasons with the Jets. During that time, the Jets ranked fourth and fifth in rushing in the league.

Wylie began his college coaching career in 1980 as offensive line coach at Brown University (1980 to 1982). He served in the same capacity at Holy Cross College for two years (1983 to 1984) before being named offensive coordinator at Ohio University from 1985 to 1987. Wylie worked at Colorado State University from 1988 to 1989, where he served as offensive line coach under NCAA Football Hall of Fame Coach Earle Bruce.

A native of West Warwick, Rhode Island, Wylie was a teacher and administrator in his hometown school system from 1973 to 1980 prior to entering the collegiate coaching arena. He played linebacker in Colorado for three years and then transferred to Roger Williams College where he earned a Bachelor of Arts degree in American studies. He later earned his master's degree in economics from the University of Rhode Island in 1975.

WYLIE AT A GLANCE

- 2006-2007: Winnipeg Blue Bombers, Offensive Line Coach
- 2005-2006: Syracuse University, Offensive Line Coach
- 2004: Arizona Cardinals, Offensive Line Coach
- 1999-2003: Chicago Bears, Offensive Line Coach
- 1997-1998: Cincinnati Bengals, Tight Ends Coach
- 1996: University of Cincinnati, Offensive Line Coach
- 1992-1995: Tampa Bay Buccaneers, Offensive Line Coach
- 1990-1991: New York Jets, Tight Ends Coach
- 1988-1989: Colorado State University, Offensive Line Coach
- 1985-1987: Ohio University, Offensive Coordinator
- 1983-1984: Holy Cross College, Offensive Line Coach
- 1980-1982: Brown University, Offensive Line Coach

Earl Browning is a native of Logan, West Virginia. He currently serves as president of Telecoach, Inc.—an organization that conducts the Nike Coach of the Year Clinics (www.nikecoyfootball.com) and produces the annual *Coach of the Year Clinics Football Manuals*. A 1958 graduate of Marshall University, he earned his M.Ed. and Rank I education certification from the University of Louisville. From 1958 to 1975, he coached football at various Louisville-area high schools. Among the honors he has been accorded are his appointments to the National Football Foundation and to the College Hall of Fame Advisory Committee on moving the museum to South Bend, Indiana. He was named to the Greater Louisville Football Coaches Association Hall of Legends in 1998. From 1992 to the present, he has served as a radio and television color analyst for Kentucky high school football games, including the Kentucky High School Athletic Association State Championship games.